# The Mighty Nelsonian

*The Story of Albert Nelson*

*Inventor of*

*"The Nelsonian One-Man-Band"*

*32 Musical Instruments Played by One Man*

*by*

# Gary Albert Hukriede

*Kris —*
*Thanks for all your help!*
*G Hukriede*

©2006 by Gary Albert Hukriede. All rights reserved.
No part of this book may be reproduced by any means without permission from the author, except for brief portions quoted for the purpose of review.

Cover art: Patricia Kiano
Cover layout: Lisa Spreck
Text and photo layout: Peter Doughty

Published by LifePath Histories, Minneapolis, MN

ISBN 0-9278294-3-1

Typefaces: Simoncini Garamond, Kaufmann

Printed and bound in the United States of America

For further information, corrections or additions, please contact the
Wright County Historical Society Heritage Center,
2001 Highway 25 North,
Buffalo, MN 55313

# ALBERT NELSON
## November 14, 1884 - July 4, 1964

Albert Nelson 1941

Among the unbelievable things that were exhibited in the great 'Believe It Or Not' show, conducted by the cartoonist Robert Ripley at the Century of Progress exposition at Chicago in 1933, was the marvelous Nelson's musical instrument, that made it possible for one man to play a 32 piece band alone.

The story of this invention is the story of one man. He is Albert Nelson who has invented the only instrument of its kind in all the world... The Nelson's band is not only the result of his musical ability but of his inventive genius as well... Many years of experiment have been spent together with a lot of practice to produce such a creation.

# DEDICATION

To Albert Nelson, his wonderful instrument,
"The Nelsonian One Man Band,"
and to his memory and rightful place in history

They say that with each person's life goes a legacy,
never to be again. So it is with Albert Nelson.

I wish to also dedicate this writing to Freddie Wright,
who kept his father's legacy alive.
Freddie passed away July 25, 2002.

Gary Albert Hukriede

"It is hoped that this combined material gives a history and background of the subject. It is also hoped that interested individuals support with financial aid the work of the Wright County Historical Society, where Albert's One-Man-Band resides."

Freddie Wright,<br>Son of Albert Nelson

# CONTENTS

**Acknowledgements**

**Introduction**
    My Earliest Memories

**1. The Pioneer Spirit**    1
    Ole and Marit Nelson
    John Olson
    Olson's Point Buffalo
    A Gathering Place

**2. The Early Years**    11
    Musical Genius
    Mechanical Genius
    Photography
    Brandon, Minnesota
    Wheaton, Minnesota
    Buffalo, Minnesota

**3. Remembering Albert**    23
    Family

**4. The Nelsonian One-Man-Band**    29
    Independent Set-Ups
    Albert's Ford Trucks

**5. Development of the Nelsonian**    39
    Operation of the Nelsonian

**6. The Century of Progress**    65
    Grand Send-Off
    Local Promotion
    Ripley's Believe It Or Not

**7. The Jay Gould Circus**    77
    Jay E. Gould

**8. The Million-Dollar Circus**    81
    Touring With the Jay Gould Circus
    Travel Journals

**9. Reedley, California**    101

**10. The Later Years**    105
    Bringing the Nelsonian from Florida

**11. Fate of the Nelsonian**    109
    Ownership History of the Nelsonian
    Next Generations
    Epilog

# Appendices

**A. Nelson Family Genealogy**    119

**B. Written Stories about Albert Nelson and His Nelsonian On-Man-Band**
    I. The Nelsonian by Albert Nelson    121
    II. The Nelsonian by Fred Wright    122
    III. The Nelsonian by Maynard Howe    125

**C. Newspaper Articles**    129

# ACKNOWLEDGEMENTS

I have many people to thank for their information about Albert and his One-Man-Band. Among those who have contributed, I would like to thank Ray Howe, who completed a Nelson genealogy and shared information with interested family members and acquaintances. I also want to thank the Howe family for all their pictures, contributions and memories. The Howes are directly related to Albert Nelson through their mother Emma, an older sister to Albert.

Thanks to Mabel Pinske, a cousin, for her stories and information about Albert's early years as told to her by her mother. Notable thanks goes to Fred (Freddie) Wright, stepson of Albert Nelson, who shared many personal stories, original pictures, newspaper articles, documents, travel journals and letters written in his own father's hand. Thanks also to my mother Adeline Hukriede, Albert's niece, and to my two sisters, Beverly and Judy, who grew up knowing Albert. I wish to also thank my cousins Wesley and Velma (Moore) Nelson in California for their contributions and family memories of Albert's visits.

Notable thanks goes to the many persons that I interviewed during the course of this writing; long time residents of the Buffalo Lake area such as Bertil Peterson, who said "I knew Albert since the Model T days", and to those many persons who supplied information about community and county resources in Buffalo, Minnesota. Special thanks go to Mr. Marquette at the highway department for his many copies of aerial views and original layouts of Olson's Point and roads in the area.

Many thanks go to Ruben Bonk for his unending commitment to the Nelsonian and the Nelsonian truck restoration. Thanks to Kris Vilmin and the many who helped with guidance and suggestions on the editing of my text. Thanks also to Pat Kiano for her suggestions and artistic expertise on designing the cover of this book.

I am deeply indebted to Mr. McDonnell, owner of the *Wright County Journal Press,* and to Mr. Ed DuBois, columnist, for their support, information and belief in this project.

Many thanks go to the helpful resources of the Wright County History Society, and all those involved with its unending preservation of history. I wish to thank Maureen Galvin and Betty Dircks for all their efforts, resources, cooperation and support for this project, and for their involvement with the Nelsonian Truck Restoration. I also wish to thank Claudia and those many others that make the history center what it is.

I wish to thank Leo and Gloria Albrecht (a grand-daughter of Jay Gould) for their valuable information and personal stories about the Jay Gould Circus. Many thanks go to Wilbur "Bud" Conrad who traveled with Albert in the circus and who remained a life-long friend to him and Ida. His original tape recordings of Albert from 1954 and photographs were very helpful in compiling this book.

I wish to also thank those many, many persons who shared their recollection of seeing Albert play. Without the help, guidance, and input of all those mentioned and many others, this book would not have been possible.

# INTRODUCTION

While looking through an old scrapbook that my mother had put together about my Great Uncle, Albert Nelson, I began to wonder if anyone had ever given him the recognition that he so deserved for his life-long accomplishment. I had learned from a cousin that a student at the University of Minnesota had done a master's thesis on Albert's invention. I knew that his instrument and memorabilia were on permanent display at the Wright County Historical Society Museum in Buffalo, Minnesota, and that there had been numerous newspaper articles published about Albert and his instrument while he was living and long after his death -- but had anyone ever put together a book about him?

My middle name is Albert. My mother named me after Albert Nelson—shouldn't I be the one to write a book about him? My remembrance of Albert Nelson was as a child less than ten years old. He would visit my grandparents in Eagle Bend, Minnesota. His machine was called the "Nelsonian One-Man-Band."

Albert did not have a formal education beyond the 8th grade. After being introduced to music at a young age, and having been taught the violin by his father and the organ by his older sister, he taught himself to play all the instruments that he would eventually incorporate into his machine. He endlessly experimented to make them work together. He was an avid musician and inventor.

It sounds straightforward. Albert Nelson designed a machine that would play 32 musical instruments together. To see "the machine" with its many tubes, wires, levers, bellows, gears, belts and varieties of hardware all combined to operate the 32 instruments embedded in its maze -- would truly impress you. If you were fortunate enough to have seen him play his invention, you would have been amazed.

To follow with your eyes the endless course of just one pneumatic tube would surprise you. Painstakingly conceived, designed, and finally implemented into bent and twisted metal, rubber tubing, wire and tubes, each item of this machine was obtained and hand-fashioned by one man, Albert Nelson. Many people considered him a genius.

In doing the research for the book, it has surprised me that although the NELSONIAN has been quiet for more than forty years, many people still remember it vividly. The Nelsonian left a lasting impression. It was truly an accomplishment and a marvel.

I had many opportunities while growing up to personally interview Albert. But as we all know, timing is a crucial element in life; without its proper use tasks usually become more difficult to accomplish, and so it was with this endeavor. Even five years before I began writing this book, if I had the interest (and time) to write about Albert Nelson, I would have had more sources to contact that knew him. Ray Howe, a second cousin has been a major source from his memories, collected information, pictures, and gracious contribution to the Wright County Historical Society.

If you asked if there would ever again be such an instrument, the answer would be "I think not!" Electronic music guided by a microchip has come such a long way, but it still lacks the richness of sound made by actual humans playing on wind, string, and percussion instruments. There is no doubt that if Albert were alive today, he would find our technology-driven world fascinating, with the many gadgets and computer-controlled devices developed decades after his death. He most assuredly would have partaken of its many wonders, and may have even experimented and developed other devices using his inventive mind. However, in creating his instrument, he utilized only the mechanics, electricity, and pneumatics of the day. He did not have the endless possibilities of the computer age.

With his inventive and creative mind he was on the cutting-edge during his era. The many early devices that he experimented with evidence this, like the machine that made it possible for him to make his own phonograph records in the 1930's and 1940's. In my family there is a "home-cut" record consisting of a metal disc as the core, with black plastic coated on both sides to accept the grooves of the needle. When played, you hear the young voices of my parents about the time of their courtship. Albert's wife, Ida, wanted to purchase a new car, but Albert wanted to purchase a recording device to produce "Home Cut" phonograph records instead. To Ida's disappointment, Albert became the owner of a new record-producing device. Displaying his usual inventiveness, he rigged the recorder placed in the basement to be activated from upstairs where he had the microphone.

After the death of his father, Freddie became the ready caretaker for his father's main focus and energy - the Nelsonian One-Man-Band.

Near his last years, Freddie entrusted me with the care of his dad's life long passion, his One-Man-Band instrument. I was the one who became the most interested, the most pro-active and the most willing to invest the time and money to preserve it. I felt honored that he had put a sentence in his will passing on the concern and care for the Nelsonian instrument to me.

This book is a compilation of stories, remembrance's and histories as told by those that knew Albert Nelson. It is a collage of sorts, with newspaper articles, photographs, events and personal interviews of those close to Albert and of those relatives, friends and strangers that knew of him and his invention, and the gift of genius that he brought to the world.

Albert Nelson was a photographer, a musician, an inventor, an engineer, and (most undoubtedly) a genius.

Gary Albert Hukriede

## My Earliest Memories

It was a warm mid-summer's evening and crowds were forming around the concessions. Through the hum of activity you can hear the periodic crash of the wood mallet ringing a bell on the High Stricker, the "barking" of the concession owners and the periodic cheers from spectators after each win. "Guess your weight, take a chance, knock over the bottles, and put a ring on and get a prize" are announced as you pass by on your way to the rides. Children weave through the crowds carrying candyfloss and gifts they have won. Others look on in amazement at the sideshows. Lines are forming to buy tickets to the Nelsonian One-Man-Band, featured at the *Century of Progress*.

When I was growing up, most summers my great uncle and aunt, Albert and Ida, would come to visit my grandparents, Oscar and Annie Nelson. Albert had a sideshow with the Jay Gould Circus and would visit, or invite us to come to see him whenever he was performing near Eagle Bend, Minnesota, where I grew up.

My mother and great aunt Ida took tickets, and people would enter a tent and huddle around the open flat bed of a truck. The truck's payload had enough musical instruments to be played by an orchestra -- only the instruments were assembled into one machine and operated by one man! The crowd flocked around this "One-Man-Band" to get a better look at its many tubes, pipes, wires, gears, belts, gadgets and musical instruments, and at the man wedged into a small seat that left only enough room to activate equipment. The movement of each limb would make several instruments come alive.

I remember especially an old metal spoon that was near his right shoulder that he would activate to change the instruments into a minor chord. His fingers, arms, elbows, mouth, legs, knees and feet would be in motion as the sounds of waltz's, marches, and music of his time poured forth. The crowd would be amazed at all the activation of equipment and the pleasing sound it produced from the many combined instruments.

One year, when I was only four years old, my mother and I visited my great uncle and aunt at the circus. Even though there was much excitement and activity, and my sisters and I got to go on all the rides free as guests of Albert Nelson, the days were long, and at my young age I got restless.

On this visit, to keep me occupied during the long evening, Albert gave me a hammer and told me in a second-generation Scandinavian brogue to walk around inside the tent and use the hammer on any fingers that tried to "sneak a peek" as he was performing. Even though there were no "fingers" that whole night, it kept me busy, and I fell asleep leaning against the back of the Nelsonian with the hammer across my lap. The music of that wonderful machine, its vibration, and flashing lights, put me fast to sleep.

On one occasion, when Albert visited our family in Eagle Bend, he borrowed some of my sister's sheet music that she had bought with her babysitting money. He was interested in all music and liked to study the "newer" songs of the day.

Growing up in the small town of Eagle Bend, I remember Saturday night was the time when all the farmers and townsfolk would come into town and do their shopping and socializing. Farmers came to buy their monthly supplies, and many groups of passers-by huddled on the streets, stopping to visit with neighbors, friends and relatives. Most everyone knew everyone else. After eight p.m. the activity quickly dwindled as everyone went home to prepare for church the following morning. Downtown, all two blocks of it, was an exciting place to be on Saturday night because of the activity and the music.

Virgil Landeen, owner of the drugstore, would play reel-to-reel tapes of Albert Nelson's "One-Man-Band" from a street mounted speaker. As a child, I remember the drugstore being an 1890s vintage building, having high ceilings with pressed metal tiles. There were large wood and glass cases from a by-gone era full of many things. I remember a particular hunting knife glistening in one of those old cases that I wanted to buy. I worked out a deal with Virgil to make payments, a quarter at a time. I was excited the day I was able to make that last payment and take my purchase home. Unfortunately, my mother did not agree with my purchase and made me bring it back to Virgil. He took it back with no hesitation and refunded a dollar and twenty-five cents.

But Saturday night, music was heard from a wooden box hung outside Virgil's main street store. Slightly smaller than the proverbial breadbox, it housed a large speaker that produced enough volume to be heard at both ends of Main Street. From either end of town you could hear the music of my great uncle's One-Man-Band.

This was the same kind of world that Albert Nelson knew growing up in the small rural farming community of Sacred Heart. These were the same kind of towns where years later he would set up performance after performance throughout the mid-west.

When I asked old timers in those small towns in which Albert played if they had ever heard of the "One Man Band," they invariably recall something about a One Man Band -- but not usually the name "Nelsonian." I suppose, there must have been other attempts during those years to integrate a number of musical instruments so one person could play them. But to my knowledge, Albert Nelson was the only one successful enough to not only blend an unheard of 32 instruments together, but also make a good living at it.

A story about Albert would not be complete without mention of the early pioneer family of which Albert was the youngest member, and of the circus, since this was so much a part of his life and livelihood.

Gary, four years old, standing in front of the Nelsonian tent at the Jay Gould Circus in Fergus Falls, Minnesota, July 1954

**Visiting Albert during his performance at the circus 1954**

**Visiting with Albert and Ida inside their travel trailer at the circus**

Albert visiting with his brother Oscar at the boyhood home of the author in Eagle Bend, Minnesota

Albert visiting his brother Oscar and wife Annie on their farm south of Eagle Bend

# THE PIONEER SPIRIT

Albert Nelson was a second generation Scandinavian whose parents had immigrated to the United States. To tell the story of Albert Nelson, one must also include a bit of pioneer history. Albert was the fourteenth child born to Ole and Marit Nelson. This early pioneer family homesteaded in Sacred Heart, Minnesota.

By the 1860s a steady growth of population had occurred in Sweden, there was not enough land to subdivide with siblings. Compounded with this growth was a severe famine, which occurred about the time Albert's father, Ole, emigrated from Sweden to Minnesota.

(To help readers understand the relationship of family members, please refer to the brief genealogy listing in Appendix A.)

## Ole and Marit Nelson

Ole arrived in Goodhue County, Minnesota on June 20, 1868. The following year on September 7, 1869, Marit arrived with their six children, ranging in age from four months to 13 years. It took her 6 weeks to make the crossing to the United States and another 10 weeks to reach Goodhue County. The ship they were on, "The Northern Lights", encountered heavy winds and storms which made the passage very slow.

Imagine the hardships and concerns that Marit must have suffered aboard ship with six children. The ship supplied some rations for its passengers, but passage relied mostly on individual independence. Luckily, Marit brought provisions such as a barrel of flatbread to help quench the appetites of her children.

Ole was a carpenter by trade. Shortly after he had arrived in Minneapolis, Minnesota, he worked as a carpenter for the railroad. He first settled in Goodhue County, where he worked for the railroad in Red Wing, Minnesota. While in Goodhue County, Native Americans were still very prevalent in the area. Women, when their men were away, would dress in men's clothing and carry a broom over their shoulders so it would appear like a rifle. The Indians would sit behind bushes at night and observe the settlers. When he milked, Ole would set out a pail of milk for the Natives. They remained in Goodhue County for several years; their daughter Hannah was born there in 1871.

By 1876, Ole had helped build a house for his son Pete and his wife on a homestead seven miles north of Sacred Heart (Renville County). In the early 1880's, Ole homesteaded land near Mink Lake (connected to Buffalo Lake by a channel) in Buffalo, Minnesota. Just the year before, there had been Indian skirmishes in the area. Ole built a sod house in the side of a hill. Their first winter was difficult with heavy snows, once they had to remove the hinges on the door in order to clear away the snow that had covered their sod dwelling. Farming was also difficult on this land. Not seeing potential in the area, in May of the next year, Ole took a job working for a Doctor in Duluth, Minnesota. They did not stay in the Buffalo area very long, possibly not much more than two years.

Knowing that Ole's daughter Maria died in Duluth in 1883, it is assumed that Ole and his family must have moved to Duluth between 1882 and 1883. As will be mentioned later, Ole's son John must have chosen not to move with the family and stayed in the Buffalo area to make his livelihood. Ole ultimately settled on the homestead seven miles North of Sacred Heart, where he remained the rest of his life.

The Nelson family was talented. Ole made

nonchalantly replied that he could not find a suitcase.

Johnny always carried a blanket with him when he traveled, and would bring his sheepskin jacket wherever he went no matter how warm the weather. At a 4th of July celebration one year, Johnny was wearing his jacket. When asked why he was wearing such a coat on such a hot day, he just replied, "If there's no fool, there's no fun."

Johnny enjoyed a good joke, and the interaction and response from others. One time Johnny made a firebreak around his haystack. He made a ring around the haystack with straw. Then while the morning dew was still heavy, he uncovered the ring of straw and burned it. Johnny told his neighbors, "I told the fire to go so far, and no further."

On his resort, one cabin was divided into separate rooms where single fisherman or a group of fisherman could lodge individually. During one busy time the resort was filled except for room 13. When one of the fishermen in a small group replied that he was superstitious and did not want a room with the number 13, Johnny told him to wait a minute and he would return. When he returned Johnny told the fisherman that he could have room 31, and the fisherman was satisfied. Johnny had reversed the order of the two numbers on the room and thereafter, it remained number 31.

During this era, community electricity was not yet available to Olson's Point. In the evenings the resort had lights, which were battery operated. These lights were powered by a bank of storage batteries, charged during the day by a large, one-piston "gas engine" that operated a generator. When Johnny upgraded the system from 6-volt to 32-volt (16 batteries), he purchased a new Delco Light Plant for $600 from a local dealer in Buffalo and paid cash. But the cash was all in coin that Johnny had gotten from boat rentals and bait sales. His helpers had separated the change into pennies, nickels, dimes and quarters, but Johnny took all the change and mixed it up in a wash bucket. Ruben Bonk remembers he brought this to the dealer and paid him for the new Light Plant, "...and it was correct to the last cent. He liked his sport."

Johnny also raised chickens and sheep, which local dogs would come and harass. One time he shot one of the dogs and hung it on his fence with a note attached to it that read: "This is what happens to any dogs that harm my sheep."

Johnny had a long barrel Colt 38 with pearl handles. His sister, Hannah, who lived with him since the early loss of her husband, had a 32 caliber. Bertil Peterson remembers that Johnny was fast with a handgun and a good marksman. On occasion, he would see Johnny at the local junkyard near Olson's Point. He remembers seeing Johnny throw a can in the air and shoot several holes in it before it reached the ground. At the junkyard also lay many discarded instruments and projects that Albert had worked on.

Another time, the neighbor's boy, Banner Peterson, came outside to empty the grounds from his mother's coffee pot. Knowing Johnny's reputation, he thought he would take him by surprise and challenged Johnny to shoot the pot in the air as he threw it up. The boy had a lot of explaining to do to his mother when he brought home the coffee pot with a bullet hole through it.

Johnny also had a reputation as the "hard-headed Swede." On a bet, he would run into a door to see if he could crack or break it. On two occasions as a young man, he had survived being shot in the head. One winter in his early 80's, he got the idea to ski off the slanted roof of the lodge house into a snow bank. When asked if he had hurt himself, he replied, "I only hit my head, otherwise I would have really gotten hurt."

Johnny was also a kind person. His wife Augusta was severely scalded in 1890. Until her death in 1907, Johnny carried her wherever she wished to go and made life for her as comfortable as he could. As written in the History of Wright County by Franklin Curtiss-Wedge about John Olson:

"A tireless worker, never considering his own health or convenience, he was never too busy to perform acts of kindness for his invalid wife. His sunny disposition has been a wonder to the community, as he has never been known to complain of his difficulties and never found fault about anything. Such rare cases of fidelity and fortitude ought to have a good influence on the grumbling humanity and help everyone to bear the burdens which appear heavy, but are light compared to the real afflictions of life."

### Printed in the Buffalo Journal-Press, January 7, 1988

"In things of a practical nature he apparently could do almost everything and anything. He was a good blacksmith, a good carpenter and an excellent stonemason. He was also an admirable entertainer for small informal groups with his shadowgraphs and with the various means he had at his command in fortune telling, plus of course the famous Johnny Olson patter.

His knowledge and wisdom were acquired entirely from experience, his formal schooling having been negligible in the early pioneer days on the prairie where he spent his boyhood."

John Olson died Sunday morning July 25th at the age of 85 years and 11 months, due to complications from a fall from one of the cabins on which he was repairing the roof. His funeral was July 28, 1948. He is buried in the Covenant Church Cemetery, Buffalo, Minnesota.

### Buffalo Journal-Press Newspaper 1948

**"Last Rites Held Here on July 28 for John Olson**
In spite of a busy harvest season a large congregation of friends from far and near came Wednesday, July 28, to the Evangelical Covenant church to pay final respects to John Olson, owner of the Buffalo Lake resort known as Olson's Point.

He died Sunday morning July 25, at an age of 85 years and 11 months. His loss is mourned by his sister Hannah, who tenderly cared for him during his illness, his sister, Mrs. C. M. Howe, of Erskine, Minn., and brothers Albert Nelson of Buffalo, and Oscar Nelson of Eagle Bend, Minn.

Acting as pallbearers were Wm. Persian, John Bohlman, Clarence Erickson, Oscar Mattson, Marvin Thour and Francis Miller. Interment was in the Covenant cemetery.

Mrs. Kermit Holmquist played the organ while Arnold C. Mattson rendered two vocal solos. The pastor of the church, Rev. Elmer F. Seagren, preached the funeral sermon, and Mr. J. Edward Anderson read the obituary with extended remarks on many incidents in the life of the deceased.

John Olson was born August 2, 1862 in Varmland, Sweden. At the tender age of seven he came in the company of his parents to this country, first settling in Goodhue county, then in Renville county and finally in Wright county."

## Olson's Point, Buffalo

Pioneer settlement of the Buffalo Lake area begun around the mid-1850's. Fred Bjork, an early resident of the Buffalo area, wrote in his personal history:

"We were the first ones to build and move into this part of Buffalo. The nearest house between us, and town was the Oakley house about 3/4 of a mile from us. The other way, going south around Buffalo Lake, we had about a mile to a log house near Mink Lake. There was nothing but real heavy timber around us, and a very narrow road to Montrose and Waverly.

There were some neighbors that moved in near our place and built homes so that made it more pleasant for us. A Johnson family from Cokato that had five children and an Olson family from Dassel that had four children moved near so now we had playmates as well as good neighbors."

It is not clear why Johnny decided to settle in Buffalo, but earlier, his father had settled the family by Mink Lake, near the parcel of land that Johnny would eventually purchase. Ole attempted farming while in Buffalo, but ultimately settled in the Sacred Heart area of Minnesota. Johnny was about 18 years old, old enough to make the decision to stay in the area, or to return to it and go on his own. There was also an established Swedish community in which he would have blended. Not much is known about Johnny's early days, but he had various jobs tending cattle on the prairie. In those days the frontier prairie lands were a challenging place to be.

Early on Johnny had an established blacksmith shop in Buffalo and also did carpentry. He would fish on a familiar point of land on Buffalo Lake just south of town. He decided that if this land ever came up for sale he would purchase it. In 1899 John Olson bought the 16 acres with 1,000 feet of lakeshore.

When he finished building a house in 1907 on his lakeshore property, he began renting fishing boats, which he did for about four years. This eventually developed into a resort. In building the house, Johnny gathered rocks from the shore and surrounding area. He

Olson's Point Lodge House 1930's

dug in the stones four feet deep for a foundation. Each of the stones were cut and squared by hand. Ray Howe described Johnny as an experienced stone mason, knowing exactly where to strike a stone to produce a straight cut. Johnny's house became known as the "Lodge House."

This point of land, on the south side of Buffalo Lake became known as "Olson's Point" and catered to fisherman and hunters from the area and the Twin Cities. People traveled from Minneapolis and St. Paul to Olson's point for the weekend. There was food and live bait available, as well as boats and cabins for rent. People would come by train, be picked up and brought to the resort, and after their stay be returned to the train by Johnny.

Fred Bjork described the popularity of Buffalo as a resort area. "On Saturday evenings we always made it a point to go to the depot to see the evening train come in. This was quite an occasion. The trains would be loaded with people going out to the different summer resorts and as they would get off the train everyone would holler - "Let me off at Buffalo." When the train left there were very few left on board. We had a lot of fun marching through town as all the people from around Cedar Point and to town would join and march single file."

By 1918, Johnny had built 15 cabins and had 30 rowboats. All meals were served for guests in the main lodge, with Johnny initially doing much of the cooking. Two of his specialties were fish soup and light pancakes made with beer that he barely stirred. It is of note that most of Johnny's boats were round bottom, which he built by hand. Round bottom boats were larger but not as common during this era.

Johnny ran a successful resort business. He was adamant about cleanliness and had strict rules not to clean fish in the cabins. Buffalo Lake had a reputation for Walleye fishing and he catered heavily to Twin City vacationers and hunters, and benefited from vacationers as far away as Chicago.

All the cabins were given their own names in addition to their cabin numbers. One cabin was called "Happy Hours," another "Noah's

View of cabins at Olson's Point with natural spring fed minnow pond in foreground 1930's

Ark" (or simply "The Ark") because of the shape of its roof, and another named "Chicken Inn." The author's parents honeymooned in the "Ark" in 1939. From immediate family members, "Happy Hours" got the reputation of being "haunted." Oscar's wife Annie (grandmother to the writer) awoke one night while sleeping in "Happy Hours" feeling like an invisible hand had been held over her face.

Wesley Nelson remembers that in 1942, for lighting Johnny had two gasoline generators in the basement of the main lodge. Two switches at the top of the stairs to the basement, one smaller than the other, controlled the generators. The smaller switch activated the smaller generator. They were turned on when needed and shut down at the end of the night after customers had left, then kerosene lamps were used. Sometimes they switched from the larger to the smaller generator.

Several other buildings were built around the Lodge House in addition to the resort cabins. Besides the barn, there was a large building for storing the wood boats over winter. Every out building had a special use or purpose. Ruben Bonk, lifelong resident of Buffalo and former president of the Wright County History Center, was amazed at what Johnny stored in some of them. There was also a red cabin with white-trim built close to the road in which someone lived year-round.

The road, Montrose Boulevard (old highway 12) used to go closer to the lodge house at Olson's Point, but its direction was changed in 1958 when it was straightened and moved farther away from the lodge house. The barn and boathouse were on the opposite side of the old road from the lodge house. Prior to 1958, old County Road 12 was officially called "County State Aid County 5."

## A Gathering Place

Olson's Point became a meeting place for sisters and brothers and their families, relatives and friends -- not only because of the resort atmosphere, but also because of John Olson. Several Scandinavian families lived in the immediate area and everyone knew each other.

Olson's Point hosted dances and events.

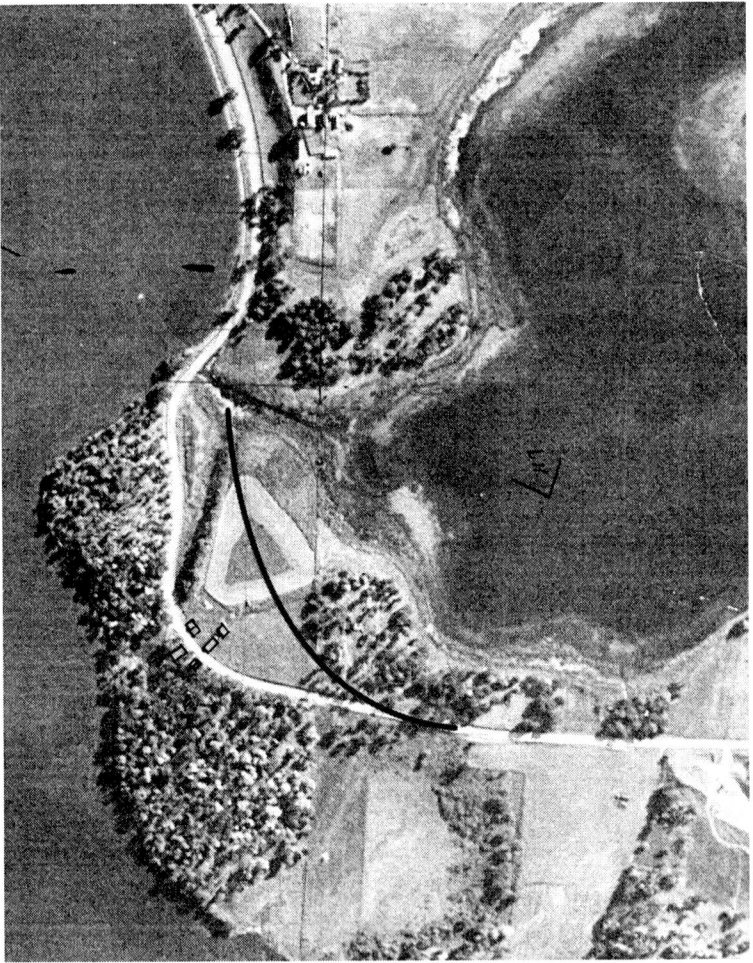

**Layout of Olson's Point from 1940 aerial photograph (line drawn shows new route)**
"Every out building had a use or purpose. It was amazing what John Olson stored in some of them (Ruben Bonk)"

Ruben Bonk remembers Olson's Point as having "very nice evening parties at the lodge. Albert would play all night. It became a gathering place."

For decades, the resort was the central gathering place for the Nelson Family. Hannah Anderson, Johnny's sister came to stay there and help her brother with the resort when her husband passed away. She has been described as a lot of fun, and a very kind person; Bertil Peterson remembers her as "bull-legged and talked fast." Beginning in 1922, Johnny's nephew, Ray Howe came every summer to Olson's Point. In 1929 he got a job with the postal service and remained at the resort permanently.

Albert Olson, brother-in-law to Albert, had an automobile garage in Buffalo where he sold Studebakers. At times Albert would play the Nelsonian in his garage on Saturday nights. Bertil Peterson remembered one Saturday in 1932 half the town was gathered around the garage to hear Albert play.

Each spring after he had moved to Florida, Albert would visit his siblings at Olson's Point to begin his touring in the Midwest. Many seasons were started in Buffalo. When old enough, other relatives, such as the author's mother would spend summers at the resort helping out.

In recent decades, and with more newcomers to the area, the name Olson's Point has come out of usage.

**Proud fishermen showing Walleyes caught in Buffalo Lake, Ray Howe on right**

**Albert displaying his catch at Olson's Point with his dog Peggy**

# THE EARLY YEARS

Albert Nelson was born and raised on a farm seven miles north of Sacred Heart, Minnesota, where his father, Ole Nelson homesteaded. Albert was the youngest of 14 children in a typical emigrant family with agriculture their livelihood. Albert's oldest brother, Pete Olson and his wife, Christina, settled just across the road from his parents. Their only child, Ella, grew up with Albert. She related information about Albert's early years to her daughter, Mabel Pinske. Ella told much of the following information to Mabel.

In the late 19th and early 20th centuries, peddlers used to come around to sell their wares. Drifters would come to the door in search of work for food, or just for food. One time Ella's father, Pete, gave bread and butter to several drifters who showed up on their doorstep. They fell asleep in the yard. From nearby bushes, Albert and Ella threw pebbles at them to see how close they could get to hit them.

Even at a young age, Albert was very nervous and became excited about things. One morning Albert, his older brother Oscar and Ella, were going to school, it had rained the day before so they had to cross the creek on a board -- Ella had to go first and hold Albert's hand. All through his life Albert was high strung, worried and easily became excited about things. Even after he had grown, Albert's nerves would give him an upset stomach.

Albert had a fear of storms. Ella remembered that when Albert was a boy and saw dark clouds approaching, or heard of a storm coming, he would run across the rural country road to Ella's house to warn them about the storm. His fear of storms continued throughout his life, especially after he had developed the Nelsonian. Later when Albert was in the circus, if he saw a cloud, he would be concerned.

Even though Albert was a cautious person, another part of his personality was also the adventurer, discoverer, and risk taker. Ella related a story when Albert was about 15 years old. One day he was riding his bicycle so fast that he lost control and fell, ruining his bicycle.

Music was the spontaneity at gatherings of family and friends. Albert saw first hand how it brought people together and created a festive atmosphere. In those days when friends visited, they pushed the furniture and rugs aside, played their instruments and danced. Music brought everyone together and kids got to stay up late those nights. This is how Albert grew up, as a Scandinavian-American in an era of heavy immigration influx. The early Scandinavian customs were fun and brought neighbors close together.

Between Christmas and New Years, couples would dress funny and go to a neighbors' house. They would be invited in to eat and have a drink, and then would take those neighbors with them to the next house where they all sang and made noise outside until invited in to have more to eat and drink. The whole group would then go on to another house, and so forth, until most of the neighbors had been included. This custom was referred to as "Yule-bakken." Stella Hanson, cousin to Albert who remembers the custom, referred to it as "good, clean fun."

When there was a newly wed couple in the neighborhood, or a significant event occur, neighbors would do a "shivery." They would beat pots and pans, blow horns, play musical instruments, and ring cowbells outside their house. The group would then be invited in to celebrate. The writer remembers this as a child himself, going along with his parents to beat on pie tins outside a neighbor's house. Unfortunately, he was too little to remember the reason for the celebration.

## Musical Genius

Albert had a natural gift for music and an inventive mind. This was noted at a young age. He only received violin and piano lessons during his early childhood; all other instruments that he played were self-taught. As early as age three when the family returned home from Sunday church services, Albert would attempt to play the music that he had heard in church. This he did on an organ that his father had made.

**Early performance c.1900**

At seven years old, Albert learned to play the violin. When he was 10 years old he played at his first dance engagement in the neighborhood. By age 10 Albert had learned to play seven instruments: the violin, piano, cello, mandolin, accordion, guitar, and organ. In Albert's own words, "As time went on, I took up several other instruments using every available time for practicing." By age 12 he was also able to play the clarinet, trumpet and trombone.

When Albert was 12 years old (1896) he learned to play the clarinet. He would sneak out of the house to practice because his father did not approve. Ole loved music and played the violin, but he must not have wanted his youngest son to play such an instrument, most likely because his chores were being neglected. Also, the violin was accepted more as a traditional Scandinavian instrument.

One day on the farm, Albert saw a goatskin drying. He tucked it under his arm and brought it to the nearby creek to wash it. He was caught by Ole. At first Ole was going to punish him for taking the skin without permission, but realized that Albert had a plan to make a drum from it. Albert dried the skin and tightly stretched it over a barrel and used pieces of board to play it. This was the very first instrument Albert made.

At 14 years old, Albert played 14 individual musical instruments. In addition to those already mentioned, he learned to play the viola, harmonica, and orchestra bells and trap drums. Albert recalled, "At 16 I took up harmony, played in bands and orchestras, and organized a string quartette."

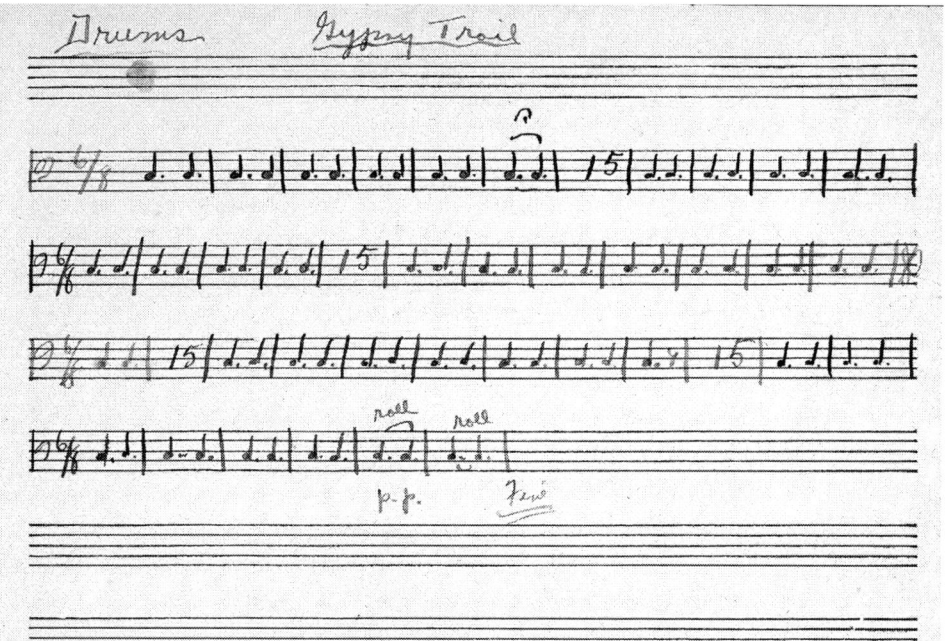

Albert and Oscar (on right) in quartette with neighbors Julius and Ole Thompson, 1900

Song "Gypsy Trail"

## Mechanical Genius

Coupled with innate abilities toward music, Albert was also very mechanically minded. Clara Howe wrote a paper on Albert while attending a finishing school in Moorhead, Minnesota. She wrote, "At the age of 13 Albert made a threshing machine for use with beans. This had many advantages over the old way of placing the beans on a canvas and trampling on them." Throughout his life he improved upon other farm equipment.

Most notable of Albert's accomplishments at this time, was the steam engine that he built and operated when he was about 15 years old. His brother, Oscar assisted him. He made the wheels and body out of wood. What he used for the firebox and boiler is not known, but it did run. Ella recalled how she, "often raked leaves to fire the boiler with, and it really did move, he could stand on it."

When Albert was about 17 years old, he visited a neighbor a mile away who had purchased a phonograph. Albert was evidently impressed by it and examined its workings closely. When he returned home, he made a machine similar to it using the mechanism from an old alarm clock. It worked effectively and provided great amusement for the whole family. A few years later, he made a larger phonograph, which was in use for years in his brother's home.

With his inventive mind, Albert came up with many improvements in his chosen industry -- photography. While in Wheaton, he perfected a vending style machine for selling pictures. The pictures were displayed behind a glass, by depositing a nickel you would receive the picture you selected. Later, when he was independently playing on the road, he had made a mechanical "Felix the Cat" that accepted nickels. As the coin would drop, it rolled its eyes and wagged its tail as to say thank you.

During the period when Albert was an established photographer in Wheaton, he built a machine for printing pictures. Described as an "automatic photo-printing machine", paper and negatives were placed in the machine and the desired number of copies preset. The prints, automatically made from the negatives, were produced completely finished. According to Walter Howe, it could work on its own and make up to 100 copies without Albert there to operate it. On the back of the original picture that Albert sent to his brother Pete, he explained how it operated:

"This is the latest picture of my automatic printing machine. This machine takes one paper, puts it in contact with the negative, turns on the light, times it any length necessary. When exposed, takes that paper away, counts it, and then takes another paper and does the same."

Albert's home made steam engine

Nelson recalled his grandfather, August, using coins to measure out his developing chemicals on a balance scale, and making his own vats out of wood.

According to Mabel Pinske, early in his career, Albert either had a studio in Granite Falls, Minnesota, or apprenticed there for a short time. He may have also apprenticed at a studio in Maynard, Minnesota only five miles from Sacred Heart prior to venturing out on his own.

Albert's 'Automatic photo-printing machine.'

Self-portrait of Albert in Brandon (26 years old) 1910

In the early 1920's he made a moving picture camera. To make the moving pictures lifelike, his 'camera' had to take 16 pictures a second. To accomplish this the film had to stop and start 16 times every second and therefore the shutter had to open and close 16 times a second. His invention worked.

Albert continued to invent and improve on things throughout his life, but the Nelsonian always took precedence.

## Photography

When Albert went out on his own, he chose the trade he had learned from his older brother, August Nelson - photography. August got into photography by accident. One day when he was returning home, he passed by a man exposing his photographic plates to the sunlight. After observing this, he decided to become a photographer. August became an apprentice to a photographer in Minneapolis. Wesley

## Brandon, Minnesota

As early as 1908 when 24 years old, Albert was operating his own photographic studio in Brandon, Minnesota, where he must have been a struggling, but hopeful, young man. While working in his selected profession, he enjoyed his hobby and passion -- music. A few years later, the two would reverse themselves.

For one reason or another, even though things seemed to be going well for Albert in Brandon, he must have been looking for other opportunities. In 1909, Albert traveled to a town in North Dakota to investigate a studio for sale. On his way he stopped for several days to visit his sister and relatives in Erskine, Minnesota.

While in Brandon, Albert purchased a motorcycle. This allowed him better transportation and extended the range of his studio, and enabled him to increase his personal involvement in playing for dances and in bands. Motorcycles were a newer entity in those days, which fit in with Albert's creativity and love of new and innovative things. On the back of the photo-postcard of the motorcycle he wrote, "Bought a motorcycle. Will use it for viewing this fall." Viewing referred to taking pictures of thrashing crews and farms.

Albert was very active in the musical events in Brandon while he was living there. He was active in local quartets, bands, and dances, and because of his talent and love of music, readily became the bandleader. Albert was also at one time in a Bugle Core that played a lot of marches.

In those days, music was the form of entertainment. Small towns had bands and small ensembles that would play in the city square on weekends, or were hired for celebrations, social gatherings and special events. They did not have the wide variety of entertainment and media available, which today we take for granted. Every town had a town square or park for groups to perform. These small ensembles were common and enjoyed by the local folk, and were an important part of the community. Albert was the bandmaster and directed several of these small bands.

Then, as now, music provided entertainment, relaxation, and fellowship. It was during one of these performance's that Albert "Rigged a cello and violin to be played at the same time", because of a cello player who did not do his part so well and would miss rehearsals. As

Albert's new motorcycle, August 1910

stated by Albert, "An idea came to me to build a contraption whereby I could also play the cello together with my violin. That turned out to be a success and for that reason I built an addition to my device and eventually played the entire quartette simultaneously. One night a wild dream haunted me to build up a whole band and play it. I immediately started drawings of ideas coming to me like wild fire."

Always wanting to learn more, when Albert had a little extra money, he would spend it on another musical instrument and learn how to play it. Instruments were added one-by-one to his creation and the manipulation became more and more difficult, to where it seemed impossible to link so many together. Each added instrument took at least two months of improving and practice. For some of the instruments, it even took years to perfect.

With his natural gift for music, and an inventive mind, the stage was set. Albert became preoccupied with the idea of one person playing several different individual instruments at the same time. Musical genius partnered with inventive genius, perseverance, and constant practice was the formula that created the ultimate one-man-band.

Little did Albert realize at this time in his young life, how this idea would absorb his energies and alter the rest of his life.

## Wheaton, Minnesota

It is not known how Albert met his first wife, but on May 29, 1912, Albert (28 years old) married Jennie Erickson (23 years old) from Evansville, near Brandon, Minnesota. As was a common practice during this time, the wedding took place at the bride's home. After they were married, Albert and Jennie operated a photographic studio in Wheaton, Minnesota. It was on the second floor of a building, located over the post office on main street several blocks from the downtown area.

Mabel visited Albert's studio in Wheaton when she was about 15 years old. She recalls, "Albert worked on combining several instruments together in the attic of an adjacent building to the one he was renting for his photograph studio. His studio was located on second floor over a post office. To go to the attic, he would go out the backdoor of his studio, over to the low roof of a shed attached to the adjacent

**Albert and Jennie's wedding picture, May 29, 1912**

demands for alimony, suit money, attorneys' fees and for maintenance, and that the findings and decision of this court may be to that effect and that no other provision may be made in these findings or in the judgment herein for any of said demands, all of which the plaintiff has acknowledged before the court that she has accepted said real property in settlement of. The court finds all of the allegations of the plaintiff's complaint to be true."

Albert's dog Peggy must have been a lot of companionship to Albert at this time. He taught her to put her paw on her head as if to say, "how dry I am" whenever he would set down a demijohn or bottle of spirits. She would also cry out on demand.

After his divorce, on one of his visits to Erskine, when Walter Howe asked Albert about his ex-wife he only replied, "Go lay an egg." After their divorce, Jennie continued to operate the photographic studio and remained in the house where she and Albert had lived. Albert and Jennie never had any children. Jennie never re-married. The 1930 census places Jennie still in Wheaton with the photographic studio, but listed as divorced and living by herself. She spent the last of her days in an Alexandria, Minnesota nursing home.

## Buffalo, Minnesota

After an initial stay at his parents farm, Albert settled in Buffalo prior to his divorce and loss of his photographic studio business and house in Wheaton, because of his brother and sister who lived there. Eventually with his brother Johnny's backing, Albert established a photographic studio in Buffalo. As related by Fred Bjork, in his personal history of the Buffalo area while talking about an Indian Artifact, mentions a photographic studio and Albert Nelson:

"Johnny Olson found a round piece of pipestone about 1/2 inch thick and 14 inches in diameter on which had been depicted the Indian cemetery and mound. It also showed the plantation of trees around the mound and depictions of Indians. It was a very rare piece done by the Indians. John Olson had this for a number of years. I personally saw it many times. Johnny had a photograph building in Buffalo known as the Albert Nelson Studio. John had left this Indian relic in there (the Studio) so people could see it, but one night this building burned to the ground and the Indian relic crumbled to pieces, a sad thing to loose.

By the way, this man Nelson was the inventor of the Nelsonian 32 piece one-man-band, which he played so beautifully. This instrument is on display at the Ray Howe home. I personally had the honor of making up some parts for this instrument. Mr. Nelson traveled around the United States and gave concerts. He traveled with Jay Gould quite a lot. It is a most wonderful instrument."

The era after June 1925 was a turning point for Albert. He was fully able to concentrate on his Nelsonian. Without the pressures of the in-laws and his deteriorating marriage, he could devote his time to his passion. He settled in with his brother, Johnny, at Olson's Point, housing his instrument in the corner of the main lodge addition, which had been added to make a ballroom. Albert became busy establishing himself in Buffalo. He continued to experiment, draw plans, and piece together more musical instruments, while also playing at county fairs, lodges in the Buffalo area, and at special events and celebrations. He had been so productive on his instrument during this time, that when they went to move it out of the lodge, they had to remove a section of stonewall. Johnny established Albert in a photographic studio in town on Bacon Street (which years later changed to 2nd street) where he worked in photography and on his machine. Major change and design is seen in his Nelsonian at this time.

The following decade of the 1930s, despite the great depression, must have been an exciting time for Albert. He had put his divorce in his past, he had re-established himself in Buffalo, with another photography studio, he had re-married, built a house in town and was near a lot of friends and relatives. Much growth occurred in Albert's instrument during this time and he was invited to be part of the Ripley's Believe It Or Not 'Odditorium' at the World's Fair. Many things were going right for Albert and he could concentrate on his creation.

In the Olson's Point area of Buffalo, several Scandinavian families had settled and were related to each other. One of these families, were the Carlson's. It is said that Albert met his second wife, Ida Carlson Wright, "through the telephone." She was a telephone operator in town. Ida's mother had a house near Olson's Point and they would come down to the resort where Albert played. Ida's son Freddie was born about four months after his natural father, Fred "Pudge" Wright, accidentally shot himself while fishing and duck hunting on Buffalo Lake. He was in the boat by himself, and had his shotgun lying near him. Evidently, while reaching forward for his shotgun, the trigger snagged, discharging and shooting him in the stomach. Some speculated about this accident, stating that Mr. Wright was an experienced hunter and should not have made such a mistake.

Little Freddie was about six years old when a Justice of the Peace married Albert and Ida, February 13, 1928, while Albert was performing in St. Louis, Missouri, over the winter. Freddie stayed in Buffalo with relatives. After his marriage to Ida, they built a house at 703 Montrose Boulevard in Buffalo (on old county road 12). The land was bought from Ida's mother on which to build the house, she lived next to them.

**Albert and Ida's house in Buffalo, Minnesota**

# Remembering Albert

Albert Nelson was of medium build with a noticeable Scandinavian brogue and a likeable nature. When he was playing his instrument, a characteristic lock of hair hung down on his right side, which seemed to dance as he was operating the various instruments, especially when manually blowing the horns.

Velma Moore remembers that Albert talked quickly, was good humored, clever and creative. Fred Wright, Albert's stepson, said that Albert could make anything or do anything. He was soft-spoken, liked the public, and was very well liked by others, but was also of a very independent nature and could be temperamental at times. Ray Howe stated, "Albert was a perfectionist and always strived to maintain the integrity of his machine."

Wesley Nelson relates, "I remember people marveled at what Albert was able to do." Gordon Stromberg, who worked at the Ford Dealership in Buffalo, sold Albert his Ford trucks and wrote the article for the 1941 Ford Times Magazine said, "There was not an instrument that Albert could not play. People would stand there and stare, shake their heads - unbelievable - they said. Some even accused him of having a little helper under the platform manipulating levers." Dorothy Carlson said that Albert, "Picked the music out of the air. If he listened to a song, he could play it."

"He was a fun guy," stated Stella Hanson, cousin of Albert on his mother's side, who remembered the visits of Albert and his first wife Jennie. Many Sundays, when Albert lived in Wheaton, he and his wife would visit his Aunt Christine who Stella lived with during the summer. Stella remembers that Albert always had his violin with him. As a child, she had her picture taken by Albert at his Wheaton studio. That is the first time she saw Albert. She remembered that, "Albert could make music with anything. He could make bird whistles and different sounds with his voice and instruments. There was music in his head, whether it was in bird sounds, or whatever. He could entertain." Others remember Albert as a thoughtful and hospitable person, he was very popular in Buffalo everyone knew him.

Bertil Peterson (90 years old when interviewed) lived several houses from Olson's Point. Having known Albert, "From the Model-T days", he described Albert as 'different.' "He always had something clever to say. Albert was very likeable and talked fast. He was always fun to be around and always livened up the party. He was naturally that way. He liked to see people laugh and have fun; he was an entertainer. Albert was also a dreamer with an inventive mind and was always joking about something. Albert was quick in all his actions, and always seemed a little on edge." The earliest time that Bertil remembered knowing Albert was when Albert had 26 instruments playing together.

One time when Albert visited neighbors without Ida, he came to see a new baby. They asked him, "Where is Ida? Did you come here to see the new baby?" Without even removing his coat he replied, "Oh, I never take her (Ida) along when I see little babies." Everyone laughed. Albert, "Always liked a good time and was always happy", said Dorothy Carlson. He and Ida had a "very sociable house - people would come and go all the time."

Albert was a careful guy; he did not take many chances. Walter Howe remembers, to be sure that he was within the 40-foot legal limit allowed for towing on public roads, Albert had precisely allowed for the total length of his vehicle and trailer to measure within three inches of that limit. His truck and trailer measured 39 feet, 9 inches.

# The Nelsonian One-Man-Band

How Albert put his *Nelsonian* together was truly amazing. He used metal tubing, wire of all thickness, items found in kitchens, garages, workshops and rubber tubing bought at a Ford automotive dealer to attach and synchronize all the instruments contained in the "Nelsonian." Many parts, estimated to be over 50,000 individual items are incorporated into the one-man-band to make it function. To activate all these devices he used mechanics, electricity, and pneumatic air pressure and vacuum.

Since the majority of his instruments were operated by air pressure, he needed an efficient pressure source. Albert experimented with many mechanical air pumps but every pump he tried was too noisy, so he had to design his own. His pump consisted of an electric motor fastened to wood and canvas circular bellows that ran silently, pumping constant air pressure to the accordion. Albert's "Nelsonian" had two pumps to power all his instruments pneumatically.

Early on, Albert had experimented with utilizing electricity to operate his instruments. Alvin Holdenbecker a friend of the Oscar Nelson family recalled, "In his first efforts, Albert tried to use electricity to control the instruments, but at different tempos the instruments would not coordinate; electricity had a delay (slow release) and solenoid noise caused by the switches clicking on and off, interfered with the quality of the music."

Electrical components were also very heavy. Albert found that it became intolerable by the time he had connected about seven instruments together with electricity. At first Albert used magnets with 6-volt batteries to operate his machine. When he changed over to pneumatic air pressure, he literally had a bushel basket full of magnets. Ray Howe remembers during this time that Albert had electro-magnets spread throughout the attic where he worked on the infant *Nelsonian*.

Albert read in a science magazine about the use of air controls in vessels, and realized that this might be an option for operating his instruments together. He went to Staples, Minnesota where they had railroad repair shops and bought an air pump that was used on locomotives to supply air pressure for their breaking system. In his early experiments to control the air pressure he used a bellows from an old parlor organ. When he was not playing, the bellows would build up to supply a steady air pressure when he was playing.

Albert had to eventually design his own constant flow air pressure system. To do this he utilized four hand-made bellows that were activated by four individual rods coming from a main shaft, which in turn was operated by a small electric motor. The main shaft of the compressor that Albert designed and built is from a turn of the century one-piston engine used on farms as a power supply. Years later when the instrument was examined by representatives from The House on the Rock, they were impressed with the speed of the pneumatics on Albert's instrument.

Bud Conrad would sometimes talk for hours with Albert when they were in the circus together. Albert would say, "I wished I could teach you to play the instrument, but even if I were able to teach you, you wouldn't have any idea how to fix it." Albert knew that there would never be anyone else that could play his instrument. He never left a manual, a "How to Book", or even many notes on the specific workings of the One-Man-Band. He kept it all in his head. The knowledge and know-how went with him when he passed away.

While only its inventor and compiler knew the full workings of the Nelsonian -- that which is known will be mentioned here.

Albert was a "well-rounded musician with a good sense of rhythm," related his great nephew Wesley Nelson, "He would do triple tonguing on the trumpet." Albert played marches, polkas and popular songs from his era. He would play medleys, blending one song into the other. He could also put the *Nelsonian* into a crescendo. Because he could not rely on reading notes when performing, he played by ear. When playing his medleys, he had to know the music by heart. He tuned all his instruments by ear and hand.

Albert memorized all the songs that he would play. Albert kept lists of song titles folded in his pocket that he would play. Using

**Pocket list of songs Albert used as a guide when performing**

most of the faculties of his body to operate the *Nelsonian*, Fred Wright wrote, "You watched in wonder, not realizing the mental concentration, physical endurance, and talent to be able to play all 32 instruments that Albert possessed to be able to operate the machine." Gordon Stromberg, when referring to Albert's Nelsonian, wrote, "The music he put out sounded like a regular orchestra, not tin-canny or artificial as some would expect." Maynard Howe wrote, "Albert at the controls of the Nelsonian One-Man-Band was a fascinating thing to see and the music rich and delightful to hear."

Prior to going to the World's Fair, Albert was warned that if someone copied his air pump invention and obtained a patent, he might have to pay a royalty to that person. Taking this into consideration, he patented it himself. There were other patents that Albert registered, including a patent on the linkage device, which controlled the bows of the cello and violin.

Albert's theme song was "Lady in Blue." While performing, when he saw a person walk into the tent that he remembered, Albert would play their favorite song. In this respect he was a real showman, and related well to his audience. Another of the many songs, which he played, was titled "Wedding of the Blue Birds." The lyrics were written by his son Fred and the music by Albert. They copyrighted this co-produced song. Other songs composed by Albert were, "Ione, Victory Bond March, Frisky, Land O' Lakes March, Liberty Bond March, Irene, Water Lillies and Erskine Fox Trot." Albert composed many songs throughout his lifetime.

Before each performance, Albert would tune the instruments in his Nelsonian for about two hours. Albert was always replacing the estimated 5,000 feet of rubber tubing in the Nelsonian. He would blow cigarette smoke into the tubing to see if it was leaking. Where smoke would escape a leak was evident.

Albert wore golf knickers (puttees), even into his later years because it was so cramped in the small space where he sat to play the Nelsonian. One arm of the chair lifted off to allow the operator to be seated. He also worn slippers so he "could feel" the instrument controls. In his own words, "I have to play the thing in house slippers because I can't handle the bass section with shoes, they're too clumsy."

Wesley Nelson remembered, Albert's bass drum had a peacock painted on it, which had "Make in China" improperly translated and stamped on its inside surface. These were the years before major trading and importing from that area of the world. Albert also had a wood and metal cat with a coin receptor, which he called "Felix the Cat." About three feet tall, it stood on its own stand. When it received nickels, it would roll its eyes and wag its tail. This mechanical device kept his patrons entertained and added to his proceeds.

Each season after Albert and Ida had moved to Florida in 1949, they continued to travel the Midwest with the Jay Gould Circus. They would headquarter in the Buffalo area where he and Ida could visit relatives. When the season ended, they would return to Florida, where Albert spent the winter tearing-down and overhauling his instrument.

Opportunities for fame periodically knocked on Albert's door, but even though he liked the limelight, he didn't like its other aspects, especially when it affected his individualism, and ultimately would go his own way - regardless of the outcome. He was his own person he liked his independence. He never wanted an agent. Albert would have undoubtedly become better known and famous, if he would have had a person promote him.

One opportunity he declined was to go to the New York World's Fair in 1939. Not only because of his experience from the previous World's Fair in Chicago, but he would not allow his instrument to be flown anywhere because he was worried about something happening to it. For the same reason when Albert was invited to be on the television show "You Asked for It," he turned it down. Bud Conrad had written to the popular television show and they invited Albert to play his invention.

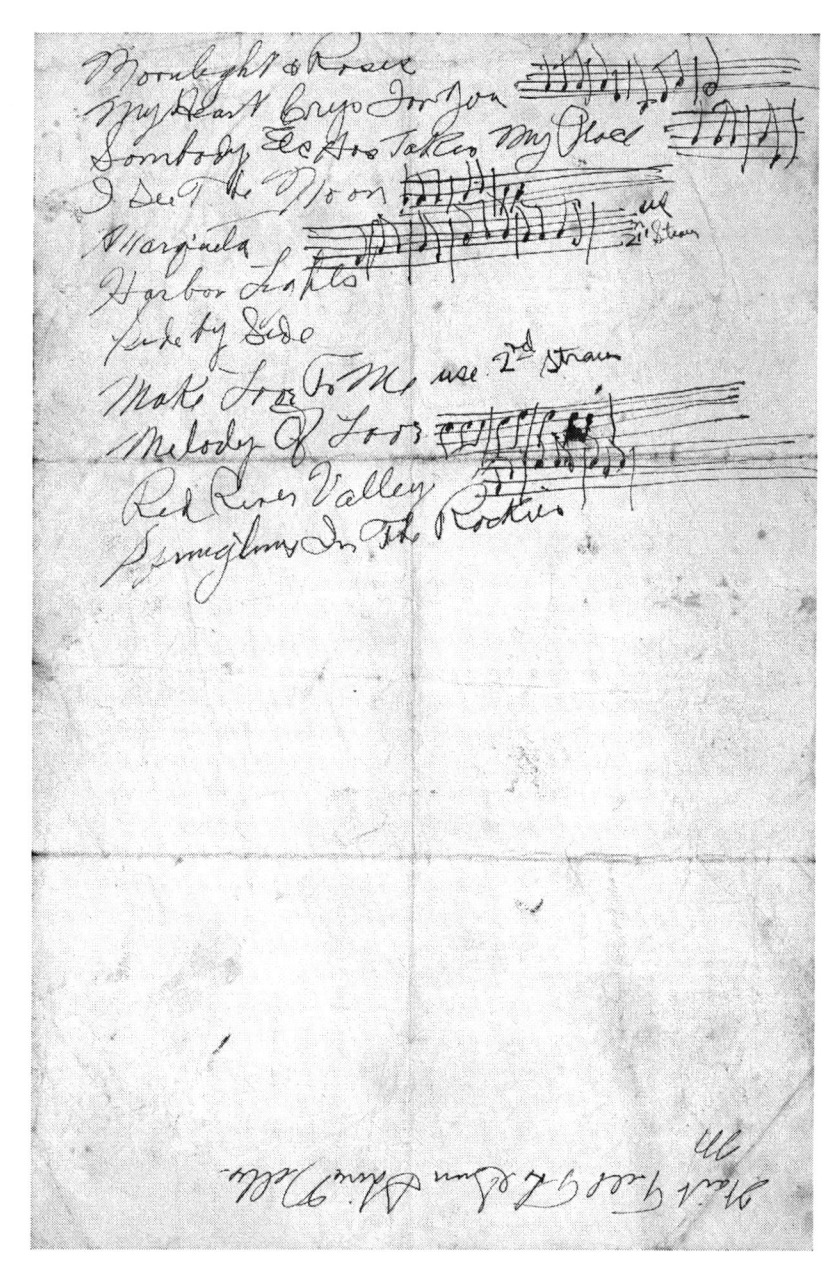

**Pocket list of songs Albert used as a guide when performing**

31

Copy of the Patent for 'Operating Means for Musical Instruments' Application for Registration of a Claim to Copyright in a Musical Composition

Patent granted September 25, 1928

"Victory Bond March" composed by Albert

"Composing"

Another time he was given an offer to perform on the Pantages Theatres network in Vaudeville. He would have received $1,000 per month for a 10-month commitment. For most persons during this era, this would have been a great opportunity. People were surprised that Albert did not take this opportunity. Maynard Howe wrote, "It apparently meant nothing to him that the well paying contract would have meant days of relative ease, with a few short appearances each afternoon and evening with stagehands to do the hard work. This may have been one of the reasons that he rejected the offer; he trusted no one but himself to have anything to do with his machine."

Gordon Stromberg, author of the article in the 1941 *Ford Times* magazine about "The Mighty Nelsonian" said, "I became exasperated at Albert many a time for turning down contracts to play at large theatres, movie contracts and various stage appearances. He enjoyed setting up in some vacant building and playing to a free audience. When I asked him why he did not take advantage of the big money, he said, I just don't want to be tied down." Gordon later wrote, "I had thought of getting Henry Ford, Sr. to view this creation (The Nelsonian), but I guess I was not 'big enough' to promote it. Had I done so I know the venerable gentlemen would have gone 'plain nuts' over it."

Other opportunities came from his exposure at the World's Fair. The following article in the Wright County Journal Press appeared when Albert was at the World's Fair:

### World Tour Planned
C. C. Pyle (alias 'Bunion Derby' and 'Cash and Carry' Pyle) has invited Mr. Nelson to travel with a troupe on an itinerary, which includes a month stand at Madison Square Garden, New York, at many of the larger cities of the Atlantic seaboard, and at several European capitols. The offer by the celebrated promoter is directly traceable to the enthusiasm with which World's Fair crowds greeted Buffalo's musician and his astonishing instrument.

A local article mentioned that Albert considered attending the 1930 International Exposition in Stockholm, Sweden. He also considered an international tour to Norway and Sweden in 1942, but changed his plans due to the war. Had Albert accepted these opportunities, he would have been rapidly launched into national fame; he could have become a household word.

Dorothy Carlson recalled, during World War II, Northern Pump in Minneapolis who did federal contracts during the war, wanted to hire Albert because they needed inventors.

*Featured by*
*Robert Ripley*

*Nelson's Band*
32 Instruments
BUFFALO, MINNESOTA

*A*
*World's*
*Fair*
*Attraction*

**Nelsonian letterhead
(above)
and
business card
(below)**

*Nelson's
One Man
Band*
32 PIECES

A CHICAGO WORLD'S FAIR EXHIBIT
ALBERT NELSON     BUFFALO, MINN.

## Independent Set-Ups

Albert was independent from his early years to 1936 when he joined the Jay Gould Circus. From his earliest beginnings when he played in a theatre in Montevideo, Minnesota to debut at the Century of Progress in Chicago in 1933, Albert covered many miles and played in many towns throughout the Midwest. He was independent at the time and relied on relatives, aquaintenances and his own promotion to land set ups. He played virtually anywhere he felt would benefit him. This was necessitated also in 1925 because of the decision he had made to end his marriage and go out on his own playing his instrument.

During the winter and spring of 1927, Albert set up in a garage on Lowry Avenue in North Minneapolis. People threw money in a hat. He received enough attention to appear in the Sunday Rotogravure section of the Minneapolis newspaper. This was Albert's first widespread public exposure.

In 1930 Albert independently set up for four days in Erskine while visiting his sister. Each day he attracted more people by word of mouth. As written by Maynard Howe:

"He (Albert) enjoyed playing in Northern Minnesota. The old Scandinavians, of whom, in those days were still many who had come from Norway and Sweden as homesteaders, were very enthusiastically appreciative of his playing. Especially when he played the old Norwegian-American folk song, "Kan Du Glemme Gamle Norge," which he produced from the Nelsonian with exceptional feeling - softly, and still more softly as some part of his body touched a switch flooding the instruments with a soothing blue light. The former Scandinavian natives stood entranced as the subdued and tremulous notes from the accordion drifted over the hushed audience."

Some early places where Albert performed with his One Man Band was at a bar on 42nd and Nicollet Avenue in Minneapolis, called

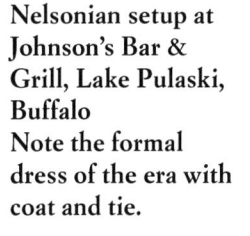

**Nelsonian setup at Johnson's Bar & Grill, Lake Pulaski, Buffalo**
Note the formal dress of the era with coat and tie.

Tinker's Inn and owned by Lloyd Tinker, a brother-in-law to Albert. Some busy Friday and Saturday nights the tap was not closed until the barrel was empty. Sometimes, up to 200 patrons came throughout the evening at an admission price of 20 cents each. One local newspaper article in the early 1940's spoke of Albert: "He drew 700 last Sunday which speaks pretty well for him." Albert also played in an old grocery store in Minneapolis.

Albert also had a stint at Matt's Happy Hour Café in Hopkins, Minnesota. During this time, Cedric Adams, well known columnist and radio personality in Minneapolis, featured Albert. Albert also played in a nightclub on Hennepin Avenue in downtown Minneapolis, near what used to be the Marigold Ballroom. He ended this setup when he realized that it was owned and managed by a locally known gangster - "Kit Cann" - Isadore Blumenfeld.

While living in Buffalo, Albert got into a tradition of playing Johnson's Lodge and Grill, a bar and restaurant at the time with 15 cabins on Lake Pulaski. Albert played there in the spring before he went out on the road for the season. He also set up in Danielson's garage in Buffalo.

Blue Earth, Minnesota was always a good booking for Albert. It was one of his busiest. For over 20 years, he seasonally traveled the county fairs in that area with the Jay Gould circus, and also independently. Albert usually played Alexandria, Minnesota near August 25th each year, which was Ida's birthday.

Albert's setups were many and varied; as long as he was able to perform and his instrument would be safe, he would play. One time, with the Jay Gould circus, Albert played seven towns in nine days. These were one-day spots with the nearest towns 100 miles apart. On one occasion, while Albert was visiting his brother Oscar in Eagle Bend, he played at a small town carnival on a closed-off side street between the town doctor's office and the corner saloon. In 1937, Albert played at Boyd High School, near Maynard, Minnesota. He did three schools in one day: Dawson, Boyd and Clarkfield High Schools in Minnesota.

## Albert's Ford Trucks

With all the traveling that Albert did, he had to periodically replace his trucks. His first truck to transport the Nelsonian was a 1925 Model T Ford. This was followed by a 1930 Model A Ford. His next truck was a 1934, on which he put 80,000 miles. A 1938 Ford Truck followed this. Both the 1934 and 1938 trucks had V-8 engines. The last truck to transport, house and protect the One Man Band, was a 1948 ton-and-a-half flat-bed Ford which Albert paid $1,737.15, less a $600 trade-in for his 1938 Ford truck. The weight of his 1948 Ford Truck was verified on a 1951 road document to be 6,890 pounds. His *Nelsonian One-Man-Band,* carried on the truck was estimated to weight 2,800 pounds.

**Copy of original bill of sale for Albert's truck**
**Purchased from the Ford Dealership in Buffalo**

| | |
|---|---:|
| 1948 Ford 1 1/2 ton chassis and cab, 100 hp, 8 cyl., 158" wheel base motor no. 88RT43063 | $1,700.00 |
| License | 37.15 |
| | $1,737.15 |
| 1938 Ford truck; trade in | -600.00 |
| Final cost | $1,137.15 |

later other wind instruments) together with a violin either in unison or in counter melody successfully." For it to sound right, sometimes the cornet and violin had to be played in unison (both playing the melody), other times, one instrument had to harmonize with, or play counter melody to the other. After much practice, Albert had mastered this. The design of the mechanism to coordinate the operation of the violin and the trumpet was later patented by Albert.

The next wind instrument added was the trombone. It did not present the complications as what had to be overcome with the trumpet. To operate this combination, Albert strapped himself into his chair where the violin was suspended in front of him. Raising or lowering the violin by its neck activated the trombone and slide cornet, which were hung with mouthpieces close to Albert's lips. The slide cornet and trombone continued to be placed just next to the violin because the raising and lowering of the violin fingerboard activated both of the instruments.

Albert also experimented with adding drums at this time. By use of his mother's doorbell mechanism attached to the arms that beat the drum (activated by Albert's left knee), he was able to roll the drums using electricity. Albert added a snare and bass drum and continued to experiment with adding other instruments -- his one-man-band was always in change.

## 1912

By 1912, Albert was able to put together and play five instruments successfully. In addition to the violin and cello, he had added a slide cornet, bass drum and snare drum. It took a lot of practice before Albert could master the manipulation of these five instruments. By this time he was referring to his invention as the "NELSONIAN."

Albert continued to perfect the integration of the added instruments and practiced playing them. While becoming proficient at playing his one-man-band machine, he continued experimenting with other instruments.

There is no doubt by this time that Albert had tried adding other instruments, but kept falling back to the five that were proven. With more practice and experiment, several years passed before he was successful in adding and mastering the playing of additional instruments. The incorporation of a total of seven instruments was his next milestone.

May 29, 1912 Albert and Jennie Erickson were married. They moved to Wheaton, Minnesota where Albert operated a photograph studio. Albert discovered an attic in the adjacent building to his studio where he could work on his invention.

## 1915

A newspaper article from 1915 stated that Albert had combined seven instruments together and was playing at various events. He had added a bass viol and cymbals.

## 1918

By 1918 Albert had 12 instruments combined together successfully. It is believed that he was able to add a trumpet, tambourine and woodblock. He had incorporated an amplifier to strengthen the stringed instruments so the percussion instruments would not overwhelm them.

The Litchfield, Minnesota newspaper at the time mentioned Albert's One-Man-Band:

**Albert Nelson is twelve-piece band. Will add two more pieces and will then get ready for road tour.**

Litchfield has a mechanical-musical genius, or musical-mechanical genius. It can be put either way and hit the mark.

Albert Nelson who came here recently from Sacred Heart is the genius.

Up to Wednesday of this week when the Review called on him he had linked together twelve musical instruments and played them all at one time as a twelve piece orchestra. He desires to add bells to the orchestra, but that will make the number 13, which of course, will not do. Mr. Nelson is musically temperamental to that extent. In due time, therefore, the orchestra will be one of 14 pieces. All of the instruments have a place on a stand not over six feet square.

Mr. Nelson already has a considerable repertoire of selections, which he plays to the delight, and surprise of his visitors. He has a little electric motor to assist him; otherwise he is the whole band or orchestra combined... He is planning now to play a town or two next week to give the 'orchestra' a tryout, when he will return to Litchfield for a prolonged term of practice.

## 1922

By 1922 Albert, having designed, experimented, and practiced on his combination of musical instruments for 12 years had perfected the playing of up to 14 instruments combined together successfully. Accomplishing most of this in the attic adjacent to his studio in Wheaton, Minnesota.

He was accepting setups, which included by 1923, the Gould Theatre in Montevideo and the 1924 Harvest Festival in his own town of Wheaton. Earning extra money through these engagements, he realized that it was possible to earn a living at this kind of livelihood. In Albert's own words, he said, "I went after it big." He received engagements at a fair, followed by theatres and more fairs and celebrations. He continued to free-lance until joining the Jay Gould Circus in 1936.

Years later, in an article in the *Pantograph Newspaper* (Bloomington, Illinois) Albert summarized his decision:

Nelson said he begin by playing in silent movie houses. Then in 1924, he added, 'I went after it big.' He began to freelance,

**The Nelsonian with 12 instruments as it looked about 1918**

**The Nelsonian as it appeared in 1922.**

**Overleaf: The Nelsonian with 22 instruments as it looked in about 1926**

playing wherever it appealed to him. As he said himself, "I went on the road." (See appendix D)

Ad bills were beginning to call his instrument an orchestra. One newspaper reported in 1924, that Albert was planning to have 18 instruments in the *Nelsonian*.

Although opportunities were beginning for Albert, his wife Jennie was not in favor of him traveling. She did not like him gone so much and neglecting his duties in the studio.

On October 27, 1922 Albert's parent's house burned down, and on December 3rd, his mother died.

## 1925

The year 1925 was a real turning point in Albert's life. This is the year he separated from his wife, moved to Buffalo, and went on his own playing at county fairs and events as an independent. He had to rebuild his instrument from the wreckage remaining after his wife's father and brother destroyed it in the attic adjacent to his studio in Wheaton.

During this period you see a real change in Albert's instrument. Being able to concentrate without distraction and with renewed energy on its design, the instrument takes on a new form leading the way to its future development and success.

A local newspaper article at the time, only mentions nine instruments. It may be that nine is what could easily be transported to engagements, or Albert was only able to piece together that number after his earlier attempt was destroyed by his inlaws. Albert was always experimenting and at times would rebuild his invention. The article goes on to give a good description of the workings of Albert's one-man-band:

The invention consists of a combination of nine instruments which he can play at one time. It consists of a viola, bass viol, cello, cornet, mandolin, bass drum, snare drum, crash cymbal and regular cymbal. The cornet and viola are played by hand and wind power. The cello is played by a bow attached to the bow in the player's hand. The bass drum is played with one of the player's feet, while the snare drum is operated by a magnet, which is controlled by a lever at the operator's foot. The bass viol and the mandolin are operated by levers at the player's feet, while the crash

PHOTO BY J.C. SEBEK, BUFFALO, MINN.

cymbal is attached to the end of a steel rod, at the end of the support which holds the bow of the cello in place. By taking a swift and long stroke, the cymbal is struck. The regular cymbal is struck by the common method of having it placed at the bottom of the drum.

Albert purchased his first truck, a 1925 Model T Ford to transport his one-man-band.

In December 1925 Albert's father passed away.

## 1926-1927

By this time, Albert had successfully combined 22 instruments together. Several newspaper articles appeared at this time focusing on the One-Man-Band and its 22 instruments that were played by only one man. In 1926 Albert was living on Lowery Avenue in North Minneapolis. He was featured several times in the Minneapolis newspaper.

An article dated November 19, 1927 (Saturday) in the *Kansas City Journal* is titled "He's working to Beat the Band." It mentions 22 instruments.

Albert was also mentioned in the October 1927 issue of *Popular Science Monthly Magazine,* stating that he had a 22-piece orchestra. It also mentions that, "An electric amplifier is used by the inventor to magnify the sounds of the stringed instruments so that they are not drowned out by the heavier brasses and drums."

Other newspaper articles quote up to 24 instruments as combined in the Nelsonian.

In 1927 Albert and Ida spent the winter working on his instrument and performing at 1004 1/2 East 48th Street in Kansas City, Missouri. Early in 1928 Albert and Ida were married in Kansas City.

**Overleaf:**
**The Nelsonian with up to 26 instruments as it appeared in 1928 Note the early attempt at incorporating a piano.**

## 1928 - 1932

Albert experimented with first one, then two pianos integrated into the Nelsonian. With the addition of four more instruments Albert had a total of 26 working instruments and continued to experiment with up to 30.

During the winter of 1931-32, Albert set up in a storefront in Buffalo, and then played at Matt's Cafe in Hopkins until going to the 1933 World's Fair.

Albert's notoriety was gaining and in 1932, the then Governor of the State of Minnesota, Floyd B. Olson, came to visit Albert and see for himself, the Nelsonian One-Man-Band.

## 1933

By early 1933, Albert had combined 30 instruments together incorporating two pianos, in time to be part of Ripley's Believe It Or Not "Odditorium" at the Century of Progress, World's Fair. The piano, accordion and marimba phone (over his head), were all activated by the accordion keyboard.

Although, Albert had 30 working instruments at this time, other variations were reported. The ad for Matt's Cafe in Hopkins, where Albert was playing prior to the World's Fair, mentioned 31 instruments. In a local advertisement about the fair, it said that the Nelsonian had 32 instruments. These variations were most likely in error, but could have been experiments Albert had tried, but did not feel that the additional instruments would function well enough to include them in the Nelsonian for the World's Fair.

One article at this time describes the Nelsonian as having over 50,000 parts and weighing 1,965 pounds.

In October 1933, after he had left the World's Fair, Albert, Ida and Freddie visited their relatives in California for the winter.

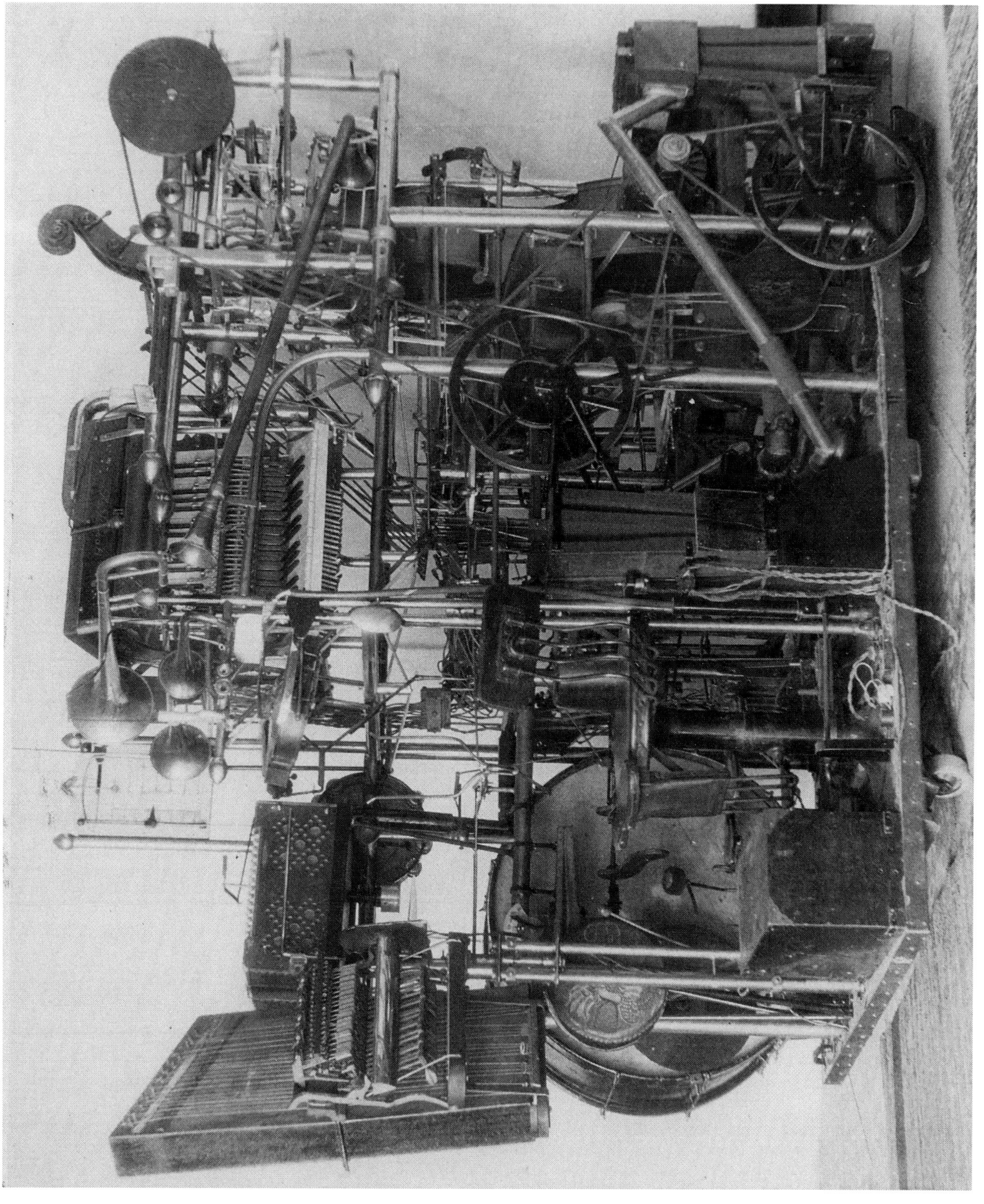

## 1934

During Albert's second visit in 1934 to his brother and sister in California, when interviewed, told the reporter that he felt he had perfected his instrument to his own satisfaction, and is now content to go about the country and bring enjoyment to people by seeing him play. In so doing, he would observe the result of his life's work. At this time Albert was 50 years old and had 30 instruments successfully integrated into the Nelsonian.

The reporter went on to explain that Albert's whole life is wrapped up in this creation and the enthusiasm of the people as they stand in awe watching him gives him energy to carry-on. He would not continue to play the Nelsonian if people did not enjoy seeing and hearing him.

In 1936, Albert received an invitation from Jay Gould to join his circus. Albert accepted and traveled with the Gould Circus for over two decades.

**The Nelsonian as it appeared with 32 instruments in 1938**

## 1938 - 1939

Albert kept two pianos on the Nelsonian for several years. By 1938 he had perfected the operation of a total of 32 instruments and music makers. By 1938, Albert estimated that he had put $30,000 into his band.

After discarding one of the two pianos, Albert added a Hammond Organ. The Hammond Organ gave him deep bass.

An article in the *Wheaton Gazette*, Wheaton, Minnesota, Friday, September 8, 1939 mentions the organ:

**Nelson's One Man Band with Hammond Organ Accompaniment**
Nelson's 32-piece One-Man-Band will again be at the Traverse County Fair, Wheaton, September 7 - 10 with many improvements and the most outstanding - a $1500.00 Hammond Organ has been added giving a lot more volume and pleasing harmony. Concert every afternoon and evening.

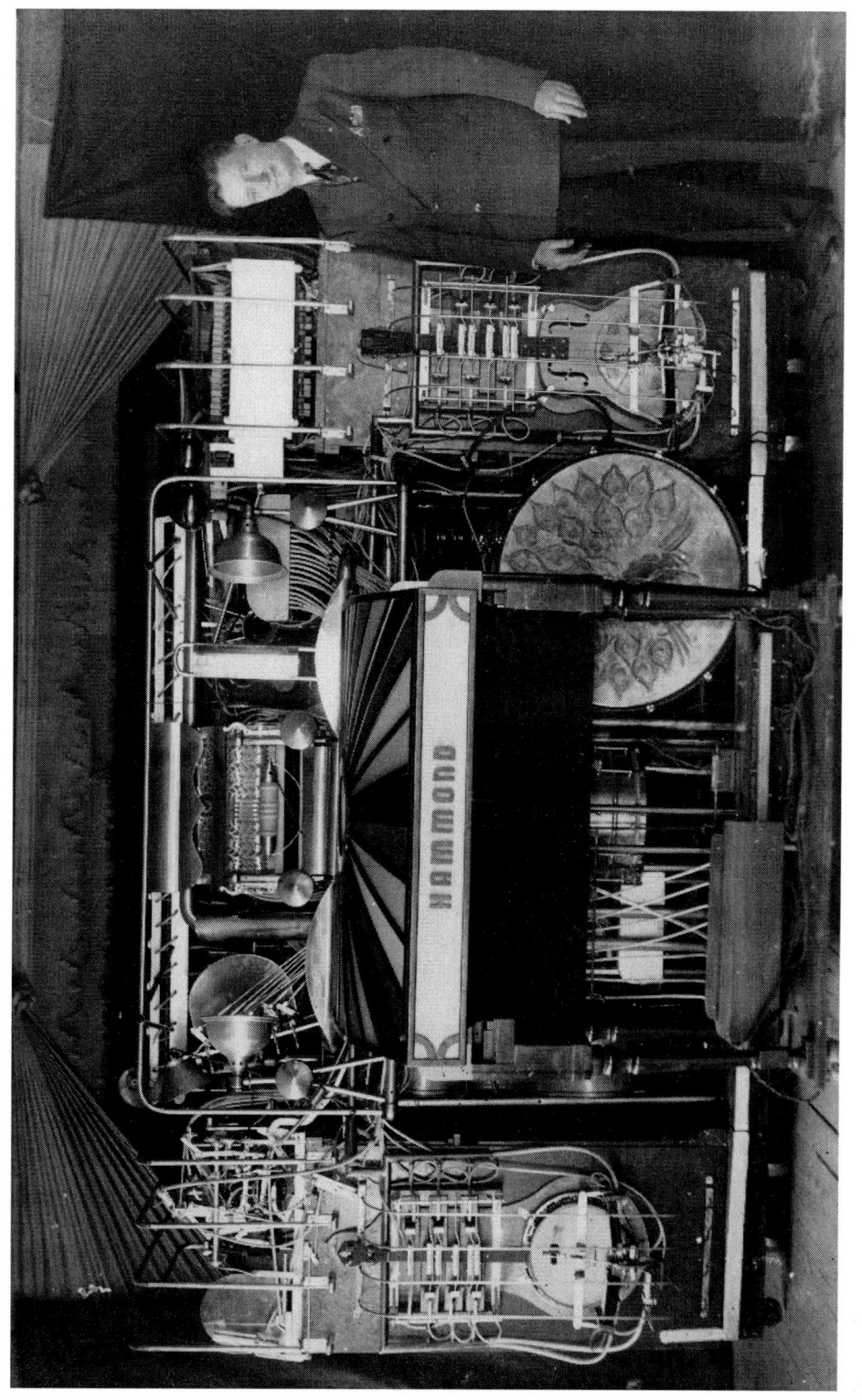

The Nelsonian with Hammond organ 1939

Front view of Nelsonian with re-decorated Hammond organ at its pinnacle of development mid-1940's

Rear view of Nelsonian showing Albert in the operator's seat

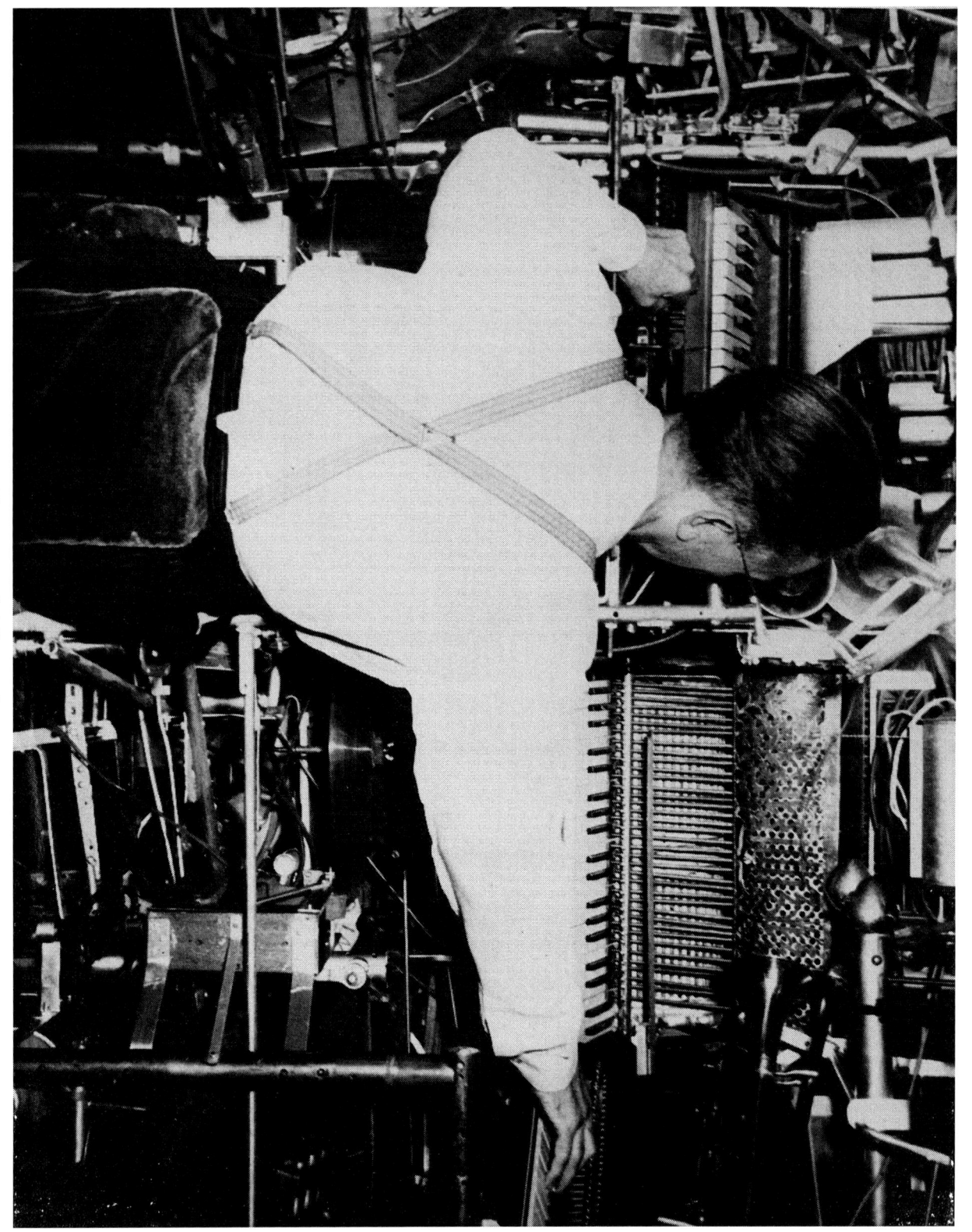

Close-up of Albert playing

## 1940s - 1950s

By the decade of the 1940s, the instrument conceived, designed, built, and nurtured by Albert Nelson, reached a plateau of development. Although experimentation continued, few major events or changes occurred. Albert could play an instrument singularly or in groups. All instruments had been synchronized to work together, but only 28 could be played simultaneously. It represented enough instruments as could be found in an orchestra. From his operator's chair Albert could manipulate all the instruments, change cords and tempo. To do this, he had 33 controls to operate the individual instruments and noisemakers.

Contained in the Nelsonian was a combination of 32 instruments and what Albert referred to as "noise makers." The instruments consist of: violin, cello, snare drum, tom toms and bass drum, slide cornet, trombone, trumpet, bass viola, mandolin, three accordions, two guitars, marimba phone (xylophone), piano, orchestra bells, banjo, and Hammond Organ. In addition are included: two tambourines, bird call, temple blocks, cymbal, two crash cymbals, chimes, siren, repeater hammer, sound whistle, and castanets. He had an amplifier for the stringed instruments, and to operate everything he had two air pumps, an electric motor and a storage battery.

By this time, the integration of the banjo into the machine had been solved. The banjo, with its cording and timing was the most difficult instrument to add into the Nelsonian. Albert toiled with synchronizing this instrument over the course of 10 years before it was perfected. In his own description, "I had to build 'a brain' in order to have it play with the other instruments." The viola was the only original instrument left from the earliest years of the one-man-band. All other instruments had been replaced. Over the years, many relatives received instruments from Albert.

In its final development, the Nelsonian weighed 2,800 pounds, and was estimated to consist of 50,000 parts and contain 5,000 feet of rubber tubing. It measured approximately six feet wide by 12 feet long, and six feet high, with estimates as high as $40,000 invested in its development.

Albert and his wife Ida, continued to live in Buffalo until 1949, when they moved to Florida. Over the winter, Albert would teardown his machine, clean it and do improvements. By May of the next year he and Ida would be on the road again to the Midwest, where they spent the summer season touring and visiting relatives and friends.

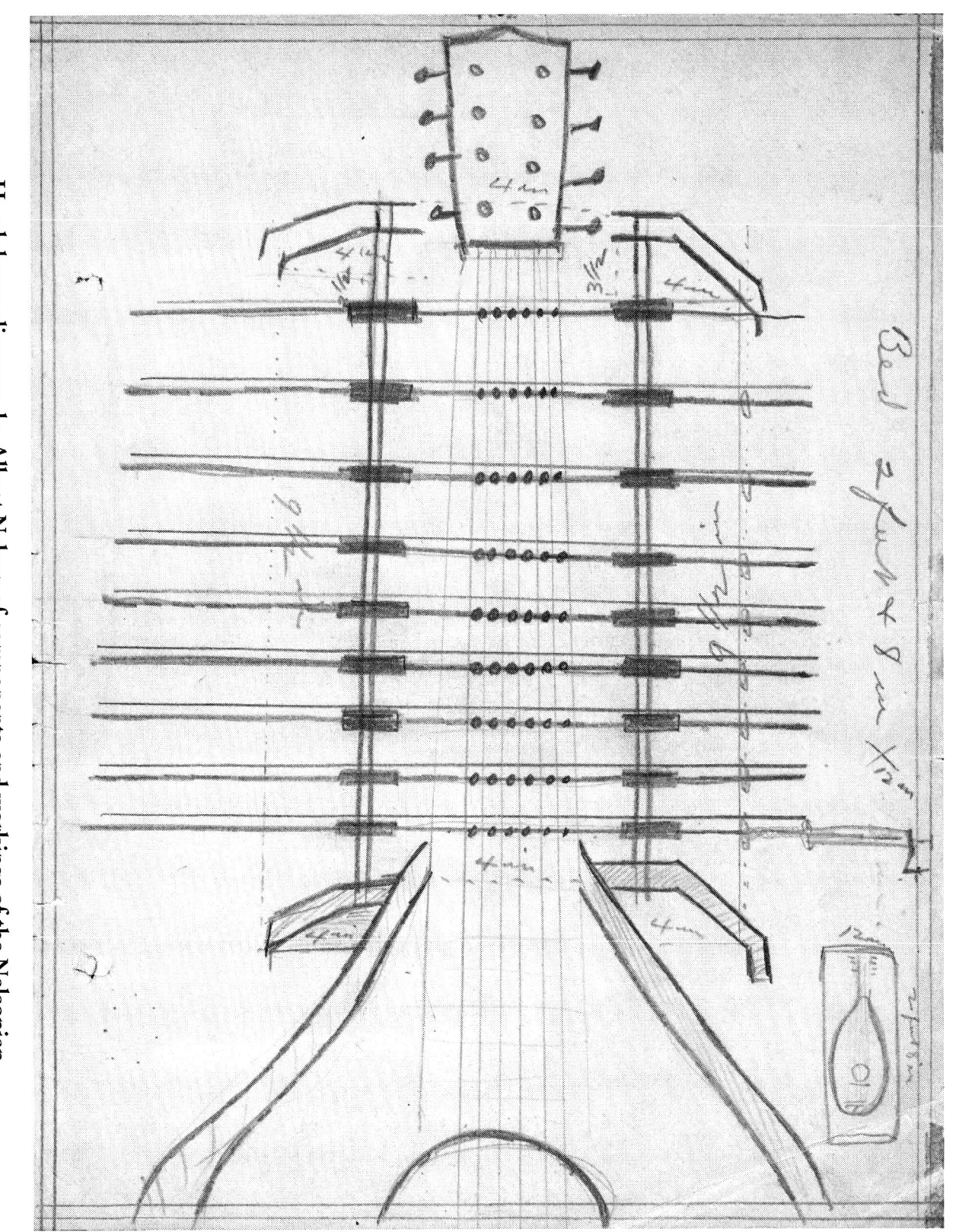

Hand drawn diagrams by Albert Nelson of components and workings of the Nelsonian.
(pages 54 - 58)

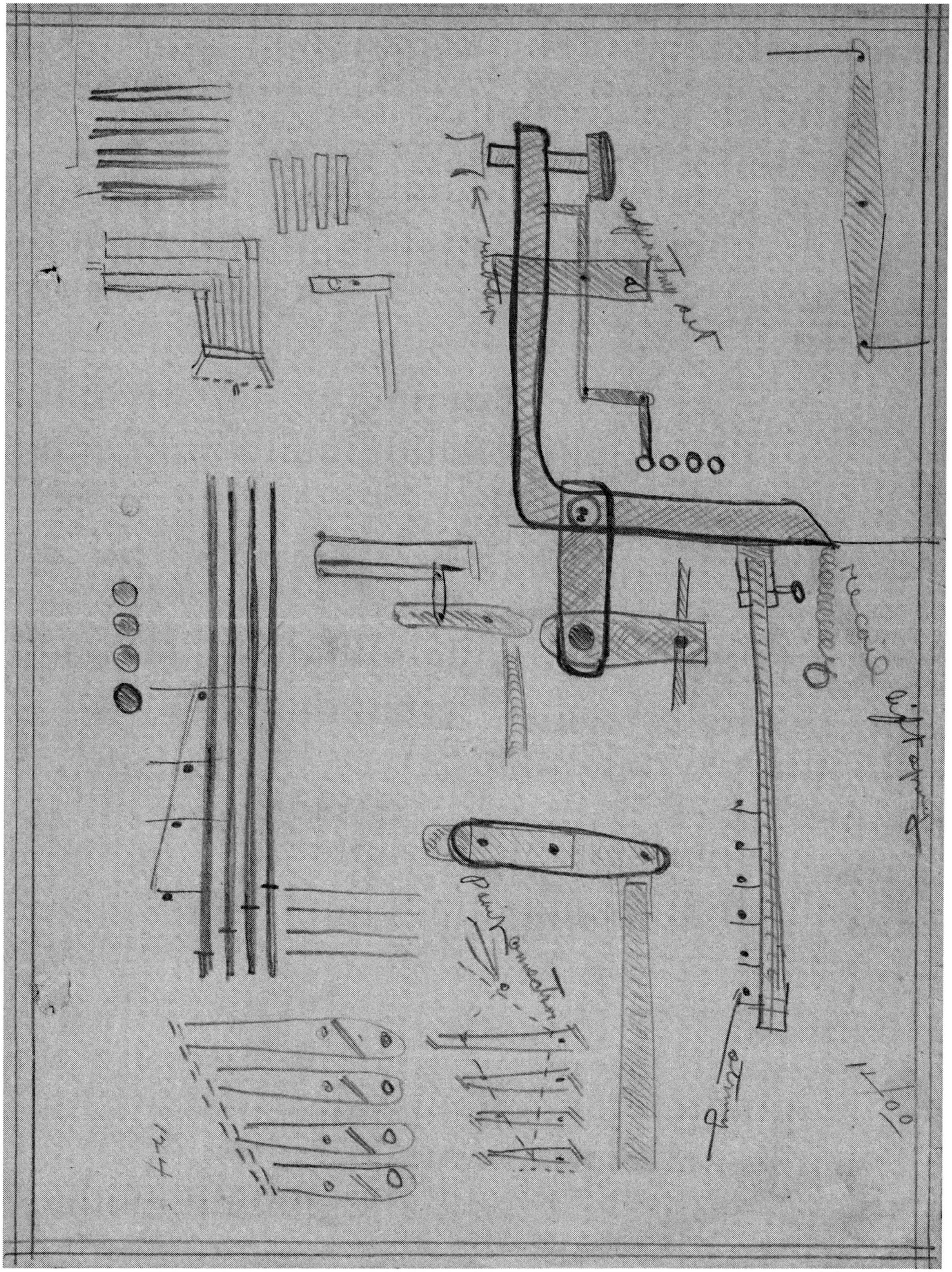

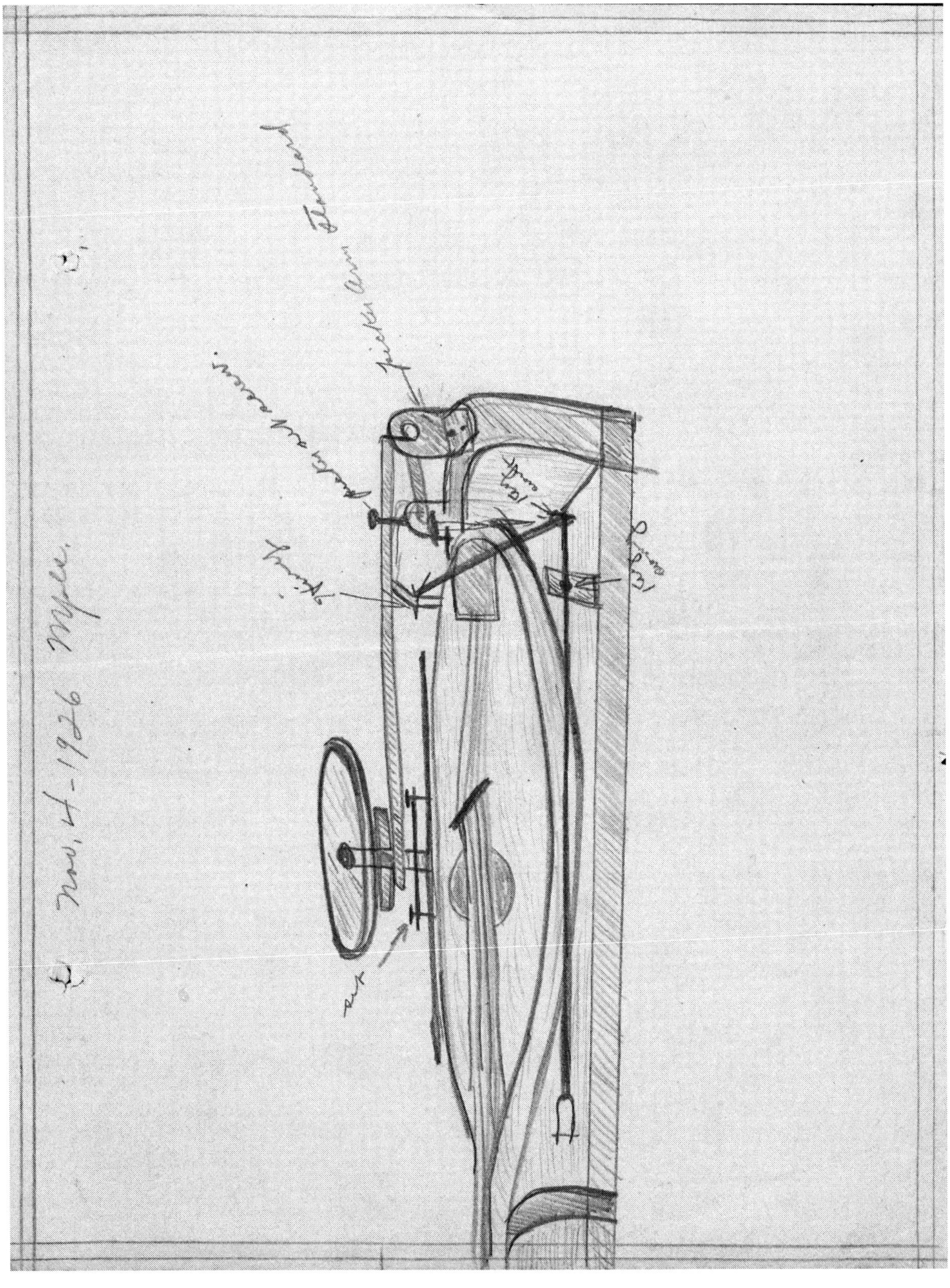
Nov. 4 - 1926 Myles
Kicker Arm Standard

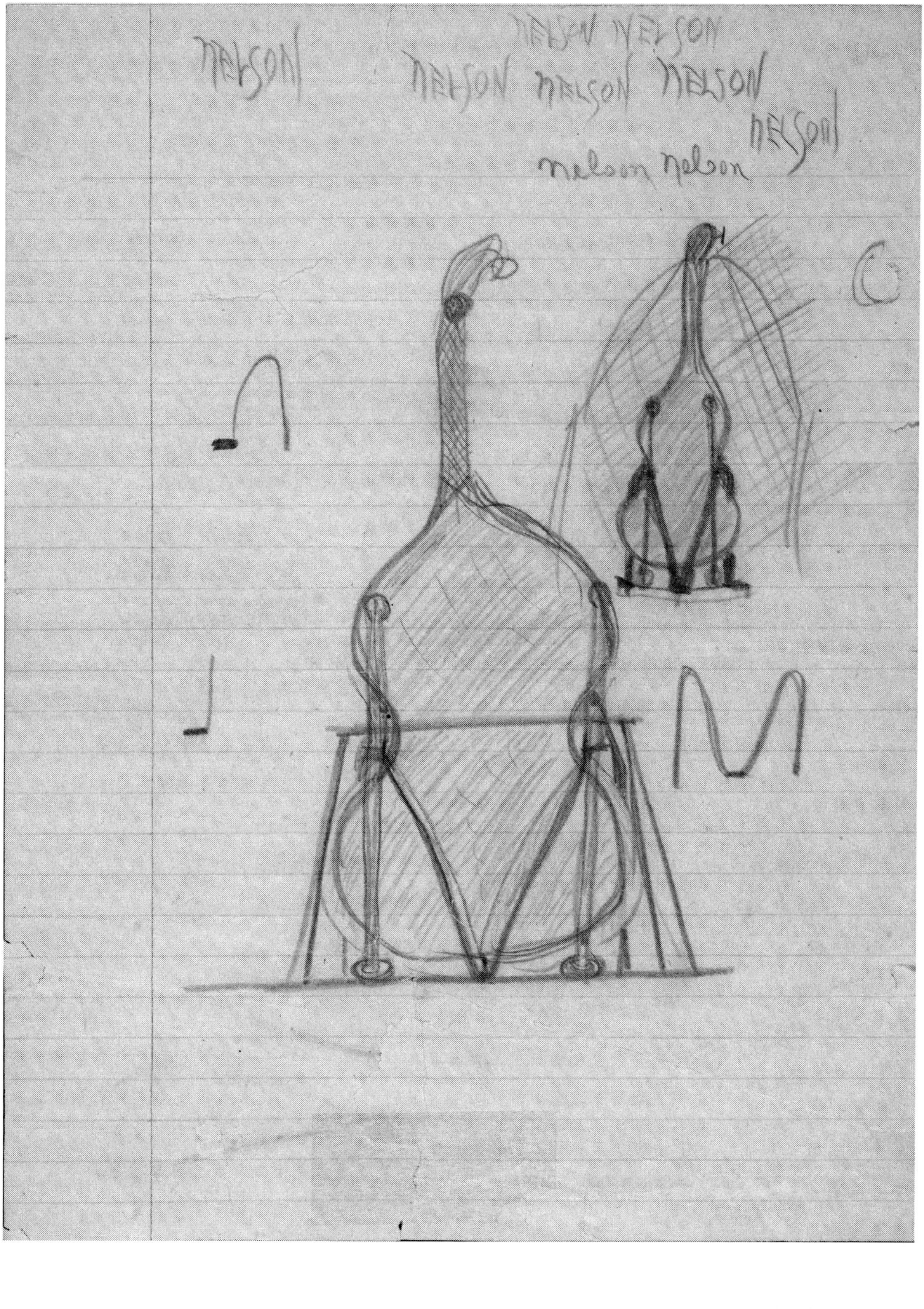
NELSON
NELSON NELSON
NELSON NELSON NELSON
NELSON
nelson nelson

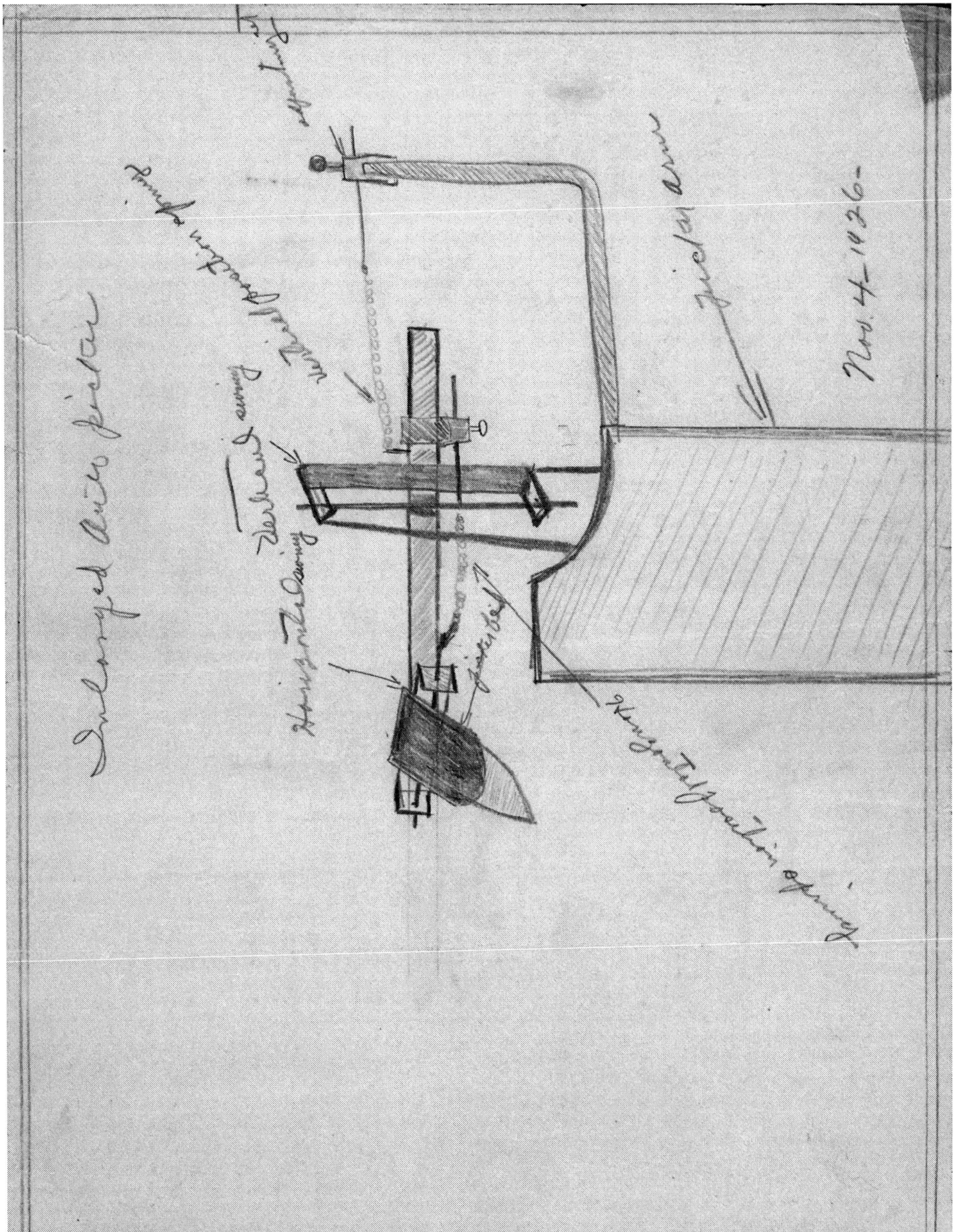
Inlarged Auto picker
Vertical swing
Horizontal swing
vertical position spring
picker arm
Nov. 4 1926

# THE TRAVELERS FIRE INSURANCE COMPANY

Policy No. **M-19393**           Agency

## MUSICAL INSTRUMENT FLOATER
### (LIMITED FORM)

On Musical Instruments and articles of equipment pertaining thereto as are listed below, the property of the assured:

| Nature of Article | Description | Amount of Insurance |
|---|---|---|
| 1. One Piano | Seaburg | $ 481.25 |
| 2. One Piano | " | 481.25 |
| 3. One Guitar | National | 78.13 |
| 4. One Guitar | " | 78.13 |
| 5. One Viola | Malmgren | 943.75 |
| 6. One Cello | --- | 910.00 |
| 7. One Bass Violin | --- | 1,037.50 |
| 8. One Banjo | --- | 126.25 |
| 9. One Mandolin | --- | 876.25 |
| 10. One Trombone | Buscher | 140.25 |
| 11. One Sliding Trumpet | Cohn | 130.00 |
| 12. One Trumpet | " | 46.25 |
| 13. Three Accordians | Rossetti | 1,012.50 |
| 14. One Accordian | Wurlitzer | 130.00 |
| 15. One Xylophone | Deagon | 193.75 |
| 16. One Bells | " | 124.50 |
| 17. One Bass Drum | Ludwig | 46.25 |
| 18. One Super Snare Drum | " | 60.25 |
| 19. One Temple Blocks | --- | 29.49 |
| 20. Two Crash Cymbals | --- | 30.00 |
| 21. Two Tambourines | --- | 23.75 |
| 22. One Amplifier | --- | 15.00 |
| 23. Two Pumps | --- | 42.00 |
| 24. Two Pumps | --- | 75.00 |
| 25. One Motor | Westinghouse | 26.25 |
| 26. One Storage Battery | --- | 5.25 |
| 27. One Keyboard | Main | 75.00 |
| 28. One Repeater Hammer | --- | 37.50 |
| 29. 3500 Feet Tubing @ 2¢ | --- | 52.50 |
| 30. Miscellaneous equipment consisting of bird call, castanets, sound whistle, drum, cymbal, tom-tom, wood-block, and siren. | | 7.50 |
| | | $7,315.50 |

THIS POLICY INSURES AGAINST DIRECT LOSS OR DAMAGE BY:

Fire, lightning, cyclone, tornado, flood, theft, and accident to conveyances.

THIS POLICY DOES NOT INSURE AGAINST:

(a) Infidelity of persons to whom the insured property may be loaned or rented;

(b) Loss or damage arising from war, invasion, hostilities, rebellion, insurrection, confiscation by order of any Government or Public Authority, or risks of contraband or illegal transportation and/or trade;

(c) Loss or damage to the property insured while left unattended in or on any automobile unless in the custody of a common carrier.

This insurance covers only within the limits of the Continental United States and Canada unless otherwise endorsed hereon.

Attached to and forming part of Policy M-**19393** of THE TRAVELERS FIRE INSURANCE COMPANY, Hartford, Connecticut.

Countersigned at Buffalo, Minnesota

this 19th day of April 19 37

_____ Agent

F-2165  12-15-34  PRINTED IN U.S.A.

## Operation of the Nelsonian

"I can get any rhythm I want. It would be hard for me to explain how it works..."
                                Albert Nelson

In the words of Maynard Howe:

To try to describe this One-Man-Band with mere words alone would be a difficult task; and to try to present with words on paper a description of the operator manipulating the intricate assemblage of musical instruments, so that a reader who had never seen and heard it could get a correct idea of what it was like, would be, well - nigh impossible.

Mechanical it was to some extent, but not mechanical in the sense that one generally associates with that word. It was not automatic. I would say that it was mechanical as is an orchestra... it responded to the will of the operator as the human orchestra responds to the baton and the actions of its conductor.

With his feet, knees, hands, and elbows Albert achieved from his One-Man-Band what an orchestra leader obtains from the various instruments controlled by individuals in the group, which is at his command. The cornet, trombone, violin, piano, accordion, and organ he played as anyone individual plays those instruments.

From its very early beginnings, Albert manually bowed the cello on his *Nelsonian*. The slide trombone and trumpet were activated together. As has been mentioned earlier, when playing his One-Man-Band, Albert used his hands, fingers, mouth, feet, knees, chest, and elbow to activate the various devices to play the instruments contained in his machine. It required a lot of coordination and stamina. In Albert's own words, "There is a lot of work involved in playing it, I have to use every muscle in my body."

Everything to activate the instruments was at arms length of the operator when seated in the chair. Keyboards pneumatically controlled the other instruments. The accordion keyboard was divided. Directly in front of the operator was a keyboard made from a segment of a piano keyboard. Beneath this was the keyboard from the bass section of an accordion. At arms reach to the right of the operator was the main keyboard, made from an accordion. From each key, a rubber tube connected to a corresponding key on the piano (located on the left side of the Nelsonian from the operator) and the Hammond Organ through their keyboards, the tubes also connected to the marimba phone and bells located over the operator. Thus, rubber tubes connect the keys of one instrument in series to the corresponding keys of the next and operate them by air pressure. Depressing a key on the accordion keyboard activates a corresponding key on the piano and Hammond Organ.

The slide cornet and trombone were linked to the violin. Raising or lowering the violin's neck extended or retracted either slide of the cornet or trombone. When playing his instrument, Albert could switch between the slide cornet and the slide trombone. To do this, he utilized a white-faced dial that he had made, to indicate the various positions of the slide. A valve trumpet was hinged to the right of the operator, when needed a manual switch allowed the mouthpiece end to swing over to the operator, when finished it would return to its normal position.

In his article, "Making Sense of the *Nelsonian*," Ed DuBois explains how this worked.

"An intriguing part of the musical contraption is a set of small bellows, which move a trumpet on a hinge. When Nelson wanted to play the trumpet, he activated one of the bellows, which made the instrument swing on its hinge to where Nelson was seated. Afterwards, the activation of the other small bellows sent the trumpet back to its special place among all the other gear."

A beveled rosin wheel chorded the base violin located deep within the *Nelsonian*, and mechanical fingering was controlled with the right knee. Using foot pedals linked to the strings at the neck of the bass violin changed the pitch. The cello was located within the machine to the right of the operator. From earliest on its bow was linked to the bow of the violin. Pedals controlled the movement from one string to the next. The mandolin was located below the cello and spinning wheels activated the strings. Because many of the stringed instruments where not easily accessible, it was difficult to apply rosin. Albert overcame this by use of mechanical rosin application.

With the drum set-up, when Albert wished to change from Waltz timing to a Fox Trot his right elbow activated a device to make the change. The only electro-magnets remaining from early experiments operated the percussion instruments.

Because of its nature, the banjo was the most difficult instrument for Albert to integrate with the many other instruments in his Nelsonian. As he described it he had to "build a brain", in order to have it play with the other instruments. His last addition, the Hammond Organ, gave Albert the most problems. On occasion he had to have an organ tuner come and tune it.

There was a bank of red and blue lights that Albert changed in response to changes in pitch. The large spoon mounted near his right shoulder, when depressed changed the instruments from a major to a minor chord. The small spoon near his stomach put the instruments into a crescendo. Right foot pedals would make the string instruments coincide with the others. The instruments were controlled singularly through cables and to groups. Therefore, with its design, Albert was able to play several instruments at a time, and then switch to different sets of instruments in the middle of a song. When Albert played the song "Mocking Bird," he would activate the wooden block, which sounded like a bird tapping.

The *Nelsonian* required a lot of upkeep. It had to be thoroughly cleaned on an annual basis. Albert admitted, "Cleaning the machine with so many parts, it takes two good weeks of work to do it." He once took out a section of the machine and it took him a week to figure out how to put it back. His biggest enemy was dust.

**Fred Wright and Gary Hukriede September 1997**

# The Century of Progress
# 1933 Chicago World's Fair

Throughout the 1920's, Albert's *Nelsonian* gained enough local attention that his fame grew. He was mentioned in local newspapers and became the subject of conversation after each performance. By the 1930's, Albert become known enough to be invited by Mr. Robert Ripley to be part of his "Odditorium" exhibit at the World's Fair in Chicago, Illinois. The theme of the Century of Progress International Exposition was science and technology and the 100th anniversary of the incorporation of the City of Chicago.

The fair extended along the coast of Lake Michigan between 12th and 39th streets, encompassing 424 acres. A total of 27.7 million persons attended from around the world. It was the first World's Fair not supported by taxes. It was set up as a non-profit organization. Relatively new technology, neon signs were used throughout the fair. Interestingly, the Star Arcturus turned on the lights of the Century of Progress each evening. Automatically each night the light from the star Arcturus was captured by photoelectric cells at the Yerkes Observatory in Wisconsin and transmitted to Chicago. This idea was conceived because it takes the light from Arcturus 40 years to reach Earth. Thus, its light signal would have been sent when the Columbian Exposition was celebrated in 1893.

Prior to the World's Fair, there was controversy if it was feasible to host such an event when the nation was deep into the depression. Critics wondered if people could afford to go to it. Despite the undertones, the World's Fair was a success and drew people from around the world. The fair opened officially on May 27th, 1933, with President Roosevelt starting it off.

Albert did independent setups and performed at Matt's Café in Hopkins for six-months before he went to the World's Fair. On Thursday, April 27, 1933, the following article appeared in a locak newspaper:

"**A. Nelson Signs Contract for World's Fair**
Mr. A. Nelson, owner of 'The Nelsonian' brought us the news on Monday morning that finally he had received a contract from the World's Fair Association for his appearance at the fair this year that met with his approval and received his signature."

## Grand Send-Off

On May 18th, 1933 the city of Buffalo, Albert's adopted town, gave him a royal send-off on the eve of his departure for the World's Fair. Buffalo was where over the course of time, Albert had built a house, had a photo studio and was where his wife Ida originated. The following articles appeared in the local newspaper:

"**Nelsonian Send-Off Set for Tonight At 7:30
'Nelsonian' To Be Honored At Great Send-Off Tonight**
Buffalo streets this evening at 7:30 will be lined with well-wishers to get a glimpse of that famous musician and inventor, Albert Nelson, when a great 'Send-Off' and 'Band Concert' by combined bands in his honor will be held at the triangle."

**Honors Paid To Albert Nelson
Local Inventor Given Big Send-Off on Eve of Trip to Fair**
Several hundred people turned out Thursday night to pay honors to Albert Nelson. Buffalo's renowned musician and inventor, on the eve of his departure for Chicago where he will exhibit his world-

## Local Promotion

Albert Nelson's appearance at the World's Fair with his *Nelsonian* would put Buffalo on the map. Each time before he played, he was introduced as, "Albert Nelson from Buffalo, Minnesota." This was a great opportunity to local businesses to promote themselves with the Nelsonian. The sentiments of the public was reflected by the following excerpt from the local newspaper:

"Mr. Nelson leaves Friday to enter upon a five-month engagement at the World's Fair at Chicago. No doubt Buffalo will receive more advertising through this one-man masterpiece than any other medium, and local folks are waiting to see what papers the world over will have to say regarding our genius and the wonderful instrument he will so proudly display and master at the fair."

Another article so aptly stated:

"Buffalo should be proud and ardent boosters for Mr. Nelson, in view of the fact that Buffalo will be advertised to the world without any expense to them."

A local reporter sent to the Ripley's Oddotorium observed that, "Of all the acts, Albert Nelson of Buffalo gets more applause at the continuation of his performances then any other attraction in the building." He reported in the local newspaper:

"Much publicity has been given the 'Nelsonian' through Mr. Ripley's cartoon and through the columns of the Chicago Herald and Examiner. Local visitors at the Century of Progress report that the word 'Buffalo' rang out again and again over Fair crowds and brought with it the nostalgic touch of a post-card from home."

Gordon W. Stromberg's, White Eagle Service Station located at the time on Bacon Street in Buffalo, was one of many businesses that helped promote the Nelsonian. Flyers were available in his station based on the story from the local *Journal-Press Newspaper*. The flyer had a picture of the "Believe It Or Not" depiction of Albert playing the Nelsonian One-Man-Band with text following.

This flyer was printed on a 12 by 7.5 inch folder with a picture of the instrument on one side and room for an address and postage stamp on the other. Above the picture, printed in large letters was, THE NEW - 1933 - "NELSONIAN." (See Appendix C)

The local newspaper kept abreast of the events through Albert's correspondence.

"Word has been received from A. Nelson that they are faring well in the 'Windy City' at the World's Fair. Nelson states that so far he has been very well received, also that Buffalo gets mention at least once every hour."

"This office received a card from A. Nelson. Everything is going o.k. Recently he performed for Amos n' Andy of radio fame."

One of the many famous people to view the *Nelsonian* while in Chicago was Vincent Lopez, one of the most popular dance bandleaders in the country at the time.

## Ripley's Believe It Or Not

The following press release was used throughout the Midwest in July 1933 by Ripley to advertise the World's Fair Odditorium exhibition, which capitalized on human oddities and inanimate curiosities. The Odditorium was the largest building on the Fair's midway. It boasted uniformed attendants, unique lighting and ventilation.

Chicago's Century of Progress and Ripley's "Believe It Or Not" exhibit have become synonymous. The display of animate and inanimate 'Believe It Or Nots' from the world famous cartoon feature in (NAME OF PAPER) has become the hit of the show.

To thousands it has been particularly exciting to see in flesh and blood so many of the people whose abilities, unusual talents, appearance, or features have been broadcast in the 'Believe It Or Not' drawings.

Now, many of these curious 'Believe It Or Not' subjects and objects are on display at Chicago's 1933 World's Fair, A Century of Progress.

The champion rice writer, E. L. Blystone, of Ardara, Pa. Who broke all records and succeeded in writing 2,871 letters on a single grain of rice, is there daily proving his remarkable talent.

Albert Nelson, of Buffalo, Minn., who is the sole operator of a modern band, consisting of thirty instruments, is another attraction. His creation was 22 years in the making and consists of fifty thousand parts. Alongside of Nelson is Singhlee, a Hindu Fire Worshipper, who cannot be burned, and places a white hot bar of iron across his tongue.

From the beginning, *Ripley's Believe It Or Not Exhibition* at the Century of Progress was an exhausting time for Albert, both physically and emotionally. It was not a good experience for Albert.

At first, Mr. Ripley had arranged to include Albert's "Nelsonian" instrument in the portion of his exhibition with all the "freaks." The area where the museum exhibits, collected around the world by Mr. Ripley, were displayed. On learning of this, Albert became upset. He said, "My goodness, I'm a genius, not a freak." His discontent made its way back to Mr. Ripley and the *Nelsonian* was moved to the main exhibit area of the Odditorium, where live performances took place on 16 staged areas.

The Main Gallery of the Odditorium was designed in a horseshoe with Albert's *Nelsonian* directly across as you entered. Spectators would enter and move along a series of individual acts and performances. At scheduled times, a curtain would open for the performance which would be introduced by one of the 'staff lecturers.' This would continue from platform to platform along the way. At times, Mr. Ripley introduced some of the acts himself. There were also rows of display cases with unusual and odd items gathered from around the world.

On-sight verbal introduction to Albert Nelson used during the fair:

"Believe It Or Not, Albert Nelson, of Buffalo, Minn., who is the sole operator of a modern band consisting of thirty instruments. Nelson's creation was 23 years in the making and consists of fifty-thousand parts."

A relative recalls visiting Albert at the exhibition hall:

"The instrument was behind a black velvet curtain. You first heard Albert playing the music, 'Anchors Away.' As the music continued to play the curtains parted revealing the front of the *Nelsonian* instrument. The stage revolved and then you saw Albert playing."

The *Nelsonian* was one of the featured performances, located at the apex of the "U" shaped Main Gallery exhibit and mounted on a rotating stage. Albert was under contract to perform each hour per day during the World's Fair. Electric fans blew on him while he played -- he worked up a good sweat. Albert received $40 a week while at the fair and Ripley's contract provided an apartment and transportation to the fair for their participants. Albert had signed a five-month contract with the International Oddities, Inc. of "Ripley's Believe It Or Not", to appear at the World's

Fair with his Nelsonian. Ripley referred to Albert's invention as, "One of the seven wonders of the world." While at the World's Fair, the hometown newspaper quoted Albert as saying, "I give an act every 45 minutes."

Ripley's was not only a commitment for the summer and fall at the World's Fair, but a six month extension to perform at various "places of amusement" under the auspices of Ripley to extend the "Odditorium" into the following year of 1934. Attracting people from around the world, attendance continued to increase. Originally only playing every 45 minutes, Albert found himself playing 36 to 44 times during a 14-hour day to accommodate the audiences moving through the exhibit.

Because of the moisture and wind from being so close to Lake Michigan, he had difficulty keeping his instruments in tune. By the time he had played about 15 weeks, it all became too much for Albert. A nervous person by nature, his nerves got the best of him. The "final straw" must have been when he developed a lip infection from operating the wind instruments. He returned to Buffalo, August 14, 1933, and a week later returned to the World's Fair to bring his instrument back to Buffalo. As mentioned in the local newspaper:

> "He (Albert Nelson) arrived in Buffalo again on Sunday (with his instrument), and plans to stay here until his health has sufficiently improved to warrant resuming his turn on the program in Robert L. Ripley's 'Odditorium' at the World's Fair.
>
> The gradually increasing crowds in the 'Believe It Or Not' palace necessitated the unusual number of shows a day. That coupled with the extreme physical exertion of playing thirty instruments with hands, elbows, feet and mouth, proved too great a strain upon Mr. Nelson's health.
>
> The *'Nelsonian'* is on contract to play at the Odditorium until November 1. If rest and the invigorating Buffalo climate sufficiently repair his health, Mr. Nelson hopes to return to Chicago by the middle of October."

In addition, only several days after he had set up at the 1933 Chicago World's Fair, the musician's union showed up and would not allow him to play under their statute of one instrument per musician, unless he operated under the classification of a "Freak Show." Albert had to hire musicians just to sit there and watch him play, because, according to the union, he would be replacing so many musicians. This added more overt pressure on him.

Some people thought that Albert had a falling out with Ripley when he left the fair that summer, but Ida's sister and her husband, merchants in Chicago, helped Albert with the contract he had signed with Mr. Ripley. There had been a clause in the contract (continuation of item #5) to allow Albert to be paid if he could not perform because of "a sore lip" or illness.

**INTERNATIONAL ODDITIES,
INCORPORATED AGREEMENT**

"FIFTH: The Exhibitor shall retain fifty per cent (50%) of the first four (4) week's salary of the Artist which shall be paid to the Artist at the expiration and fulfillment of this agreement, and should the Artist fail to appear at any performance or fail to abide by all the rules and regulations set forth governing the Artist's appearances the Exhibitor has a right to retain any moneys due the Artist as liquidated damages." (Signed, May 8, 1933)

A separate cut out strip was attached to the original contract stating the following:

This addenda is a continuation of Clause 5:

Unless the artist has a sore lip or is sick and has been examined by Exhibitor's physician, in which case the Exhibitor is

THE
ONE MAN BAND
OF 50,000 PARTS

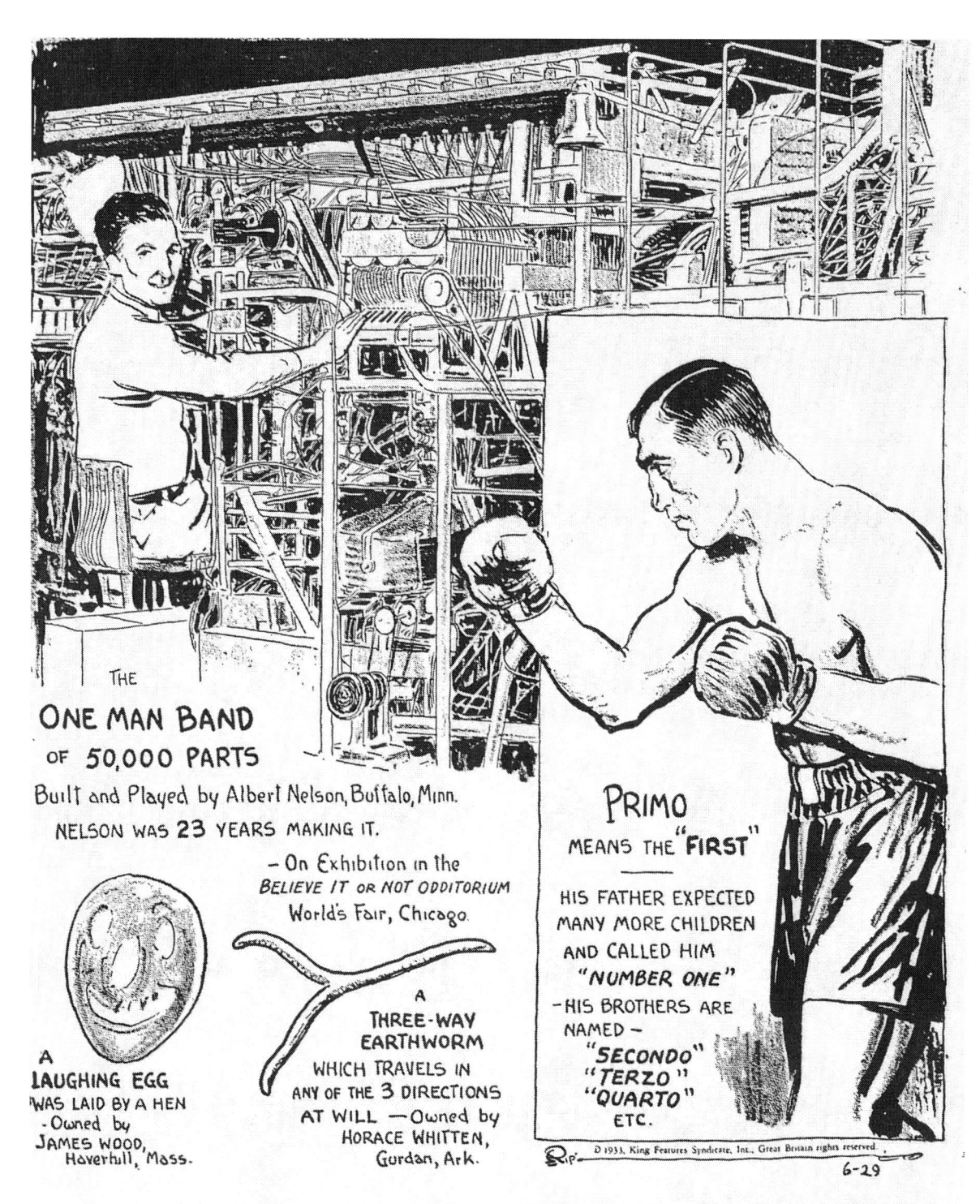

Built and Played by Albert Nelson, Buffalo, Minn.
NELSON WAS 23 YEARS MAKING IT.

— On Exhibition in the
BELIEVE IT OR NOT ODDITORIUM
World's Fair, Chicago.

A
LAUGHING EGG
WAS LAID BY A HEN
— Owned by
JAMES WOOD,
Haverhill, Mass.

A
THREE-WAY
EARTHWORM
WHICH TRAVELS IN
ANY OF THE 3 DIRECTIONS
AT WILL — Owned by
HORACE WHITTEN,
Gurdan, Ark.

PRIMO
MEANS THE "FIRST"

HIS FATHER EXPECTED
MANY MORE CHILDREN
AND CALLED HIM
"NUMBER ONE"
— HIS BROTHERS ARE
NAMED —
"SECONDO"
"TERZO"
"QUARTO"
ETC.

D 1933, King Features Syndicate, Inc., Great Britain rights reserved.
6-29

©RIPLEY'S BELIEVE IT OR NOT!
WORLD RIGHTS RESERVED, 1933.

Ripley's Believe It Or Not cartoon showing Albert and the Nelsonian

## INTERNATIONAL ODDITIES, INCORPORATED
### 666 Lake Shore Drive
### Chicago, Illinois

# AGREEMENT

THIS AGREEMENT made and entered into this 5TH day of MAY, A. D. 19 33, by and between INTERNATIONAL ODDITIES, INCORPORATED, an Illinois Corporation, of Chicago, Illinois, hereinafter designated as the "Exhibitor," and ALBERT NELSON, whose permanent address is _____ Street, City of BUFFALO, State of MINNESOTA, the act or attraction known as MECHANICAL ONE-MAN BAND -21 PIECES hereinafter designated as the "Artist," WITNESSETH:

WHEREAS, said Exhibitor is engaged in exhibiting attractions known as RIPLEY'S "BELIEVE-IT-OR-NOT" EXHIBITION, at A CENTURY OF PROGRESS, Chicago, Illinois, and,

WHEREAS, said Artist is desirous of performing and exhibiting his or her attraction during A CENTURY OF PROGRESS, in Chicago, Illinois,

NOW, THEREFORE, in consideration of One Dollar and other good and valuable considerations, receipt whereof is hereby acknowledged, and the mutual agreements and promises hereinafter contained, and the said parties hereto agree as follows:

FIRST: The Exhibitor hereby engages the sole and exclusive services of the Artist for the period from June 1, 1933, to October 31, 1933, or until such time as A CENTURY OF PROGRESS 1933 shall remain open to the public and the Artist hereby agrees to render his sole and exclusive services for the Exhibitor during said period of time at Chicago, Illinois, during A CENTURY OF PROGRESS 1933. It is further agreed that the Artist shall report to the Exhibitor at Chicago, Illinois, at least six (6) days before the opening date for RIPLEY'S "BELIEVE-IT-OR-NOT" EXHIBITION, but in the event that said opening date of said EXHIBITION shall be later than June 1, 1933, the Exhibitor agrees to give notice to the Artist of the exact date to report to Chicago, Illinois, not later than May 20, 1933.

SECOND: The Exhibitor agrees to pay the Artist FORTY ($40.00) dollars per week for each and every week that said Artist shall perform, and it is understood and agreed that one week as used herein shall be construed herein as seven days, and said Artist agrees to exhibit and perform at all times while the RIPLEY'S "BELIEVE-IT-OR-NOT" EXHIBITION remains open to the public.

THIRD: The Exhibitor agrees to furnish the Artist with transportation to and from his destination and also to furnish Artist with lodging and meals during the period of this agreement.

FOURTH: The Exhibitor has the privilege of cancelling this agreement by giving the Artist a two weeks' notice in writing by registered mail.

FIFTH: The Exhibitor shall retain fifty per cent (50%) of the first four (4) weeks' salary of the Artist which shall be paid to the Artist at the expiration and fulfillment of this agreement, and should the Artist fail to appear at any performance or fail to abide by all the rules and regulations set forth governing the Artist's appearances the Exhibitor has a right to retain any moneys due the Artist as liquidated damages.

**This addenda is a continuation of Clause 5:**
**Unless the artist has a sore lip or is sick and has been examined by Exhibitor's physician, in which case the Exhibitor is not to retain any moneys due the Artist as liquidated damages.**

agrees to furnish the Exhibitor with six (6) different poses of photographs, together with a biographical sketch of his or her life, immediately upon the signing of this agreement.

EIGHTH: It is expressly understood and agreed that the Exhibitor has the exclusive right and privilege of advertising and publicizing said Artist and the complete right to sell publications, biographies and descriptions of the Artist in any printed form and the right to include such publications, biographies and/or descriptions in any printed pamphlet or book either before the duration of this contract or at any time thereafter, and further that the Artist is under the exclusive management and control of the Exhibitor during the period of this agreement or any extension thereof.

NINTH: If the said Exhibitor shall be unable to perform any of its obligations under this contract by reason of fires, strikes or damage by the elements or of any unavoidable casualty beyond the control of said Exhibitor, then such obligations on the part of such Exhibitor shall at once terminate and cease at the option of the Exhibitor.

It is further agreed by and between the Exhibitor and the Artist that the Exhibitor shall in no event be held liable or responsible for any loss of or damage to any property of the Artist nor for any injuries sustained by said Artist, and the Artist hereby releases the Exhibitor from any and all claims for liability on account thereof during the period of this contract.

IN WITNESS WHEREOF the said Exhibitor has caused this agreement to be executed and said Artist has hereunto set _____ hand and seal the day and year first above written.

Subscribed and sworn to before me this 8th day of May 1933

*Geo. W. Anderson*
GEO. W. ANDERSON,
Notary Public, Wright County, Minn.

INTERNATIONAL ODDITIES, INCORPORATED
By *Chas C Ryo*

x *Albert Nelson* (SEAL)

*Albert's Signed Contract*

not to retain any moneys due the Artist as liquidated damages."

As mentioned earlier, Albert had signed a contract to play for Ripley from June 1st to October 31st, 1933, the duration of the World's Fair. The contract also included commitment to Ripley's engagements to be performed during the next year, thus extending his Odditorium to other areas of the United States.

With the help and guidance of his merchant brother-in-law in Chicago, Albert was able to reach an agreement with Mr. Ripley. Based on the agreement reached, Ripley would not allow Albert to play publicly anywhere during the rest of the summer. Albert received full compensation of his salary earned, a total of $600 for the time that he had spent at the World's Fair.

When Albert left *Ripley's Believe It Or Not Odditorium*, at the World's Fair, a Roy Gardner took his place. Mr. Gardner played an instrument with 80 pipes and strings, which took three hours a day to tune.

After his return from the World's Fair, when asked about his experience, Albert said that he would never again play for such an event. Walter Howe remembers Albert telling him that, "He would never again play in a World's Fair." A friend of the family, when he first met Albert at Oscar's farm in Eagle Bend in 1934, remembered that Albert was still healing from the lip infection developed at the Chicago World's Fair.

The opportunity of playing at the World's Fair, gave Albert much exposure. Over 27 million people, representing 300 hundred newspapers worldwide and people from 42 countries, speaking 17 languages, attended the fair. Thousands from around the world saw Albert play, even in the short time that he was at the Fair. Postcards were also sold promoting the various featured exhibits and performances. The *Nelsonian* was highlighted as one of these.

The following year 1934, Buffalo presented Albert with a neon sign in gratitude of his involvement in the World's Fair and the exposure it gave the city through his exhibit. The following article from the *Wright County Journal Press,* October 26, 1934 describes the event.

**New Neon Sign To Light Up Nelsonian**
Buffalo's famed musician, inventor of the Thirty Piece One Man Band will be honored at the high school auditorium here Friday night, Oct. 26.

In the meantime, officers of the Junior Ass'n of Commerce and other local citizens raised a fund with which to purchase a Neon Electric Sign, reading:

'Nelsonian Buffalo, Minn.' this sign will be presented to Mr. Nelson.

In addition a very good program has been arranged for 8 p.m. Friday night. The school band will also furnish music. The public is requested to be present and show their appreciation toward the Nelsonian. There will be no admission charge.

**CARD OF THANKS**
We wish to thank our many friends and the Junior Association of Commerce of Buffalo and all those who were responsible for the wonderful Neon Sign that was presented to us. We also want to extend our thanks for the splendid program held in our honor at the High School Auditorium. We assure you that this event will never be forgotten.
Mr. And Mrs. Albert Nelson, "The *Nelsonian*."

Despite the events of the Century of Progress, Ripley invited Albert to the New York World's Fair by a personal telegram. Although stipulation was that Albert was going to be part of this

**WESTERN UNION**

62 AS 65 DL 4 EXTRA NEW YORK NY 1201P JAN 17 1936

ALBERT NELSON
BUFFTO MINN

ADVISE IF RUBEY COMAN CALLED TO SEE YOU ALSO WIRE ME IF YOU WILL ACCEPT A TOUR SPONSERED BY RIPLEY IN THEATRES NEVER OVER SIX SHOWS DAILY ADVISE LOWEST SALARY PLUS TRANSPORTATION INCLUDE IN ANSWER BOOKING FEE THIS OFFICE EQUIVALENT SUM TEN PER CENT ARE YOU IN CONDITION TO APPEAR AND PLAY YOUR INSTRUMENT ADVISE BY WESTERN UNION WHEN YOU CAN ARRIVE NEW YORK.

RUSH JERMON
GLOBE THEATRE BLDG NEW YORK

Telegram received from Ripley

event, even a newspaper article appeared to the effect, Albert never did commit to it.

In 1939 the local newspaper printed an article headlined, "Nelson at N. Y. Fair?"

"Albert Nelson of Buffalo may provide the New York World's Fair with one of America's freak musical instruments should he decide to fill an engagement which he is now considering."

As his fame grew, Albert received many offers from various groups, organizations, businesses and individuals, especially after his exposure from the Century of Progress. Years after the World's Fair, Albert used the experience in promoting his *Nelsonian*. He would readily admit, "Ripley got me started in the big time."

# THE JAY GOULD CIRCUS

**A story about Albert Nelson would not be complete without mention of the circus, since this was so much a part of his life and livelihood.**

Jay Gould (1886-1967), founder of the Million Dollar Circus is one of Minnesota's greatest showmen. He is included in the Circus Hall of Fame, in Sarasota, Florida. Former circus members describe him as a wonderful and brilliant man. He looked very distinguished as he came out to announce the start of the circus. He wore a white suite with a Homburg hat and a red carnation boutonniere; these were his trademarks. Jay Gould was Master of Ceremonies for his own performances. A very strict and religious man, he would hold his hat to his chest and say a prayer before the start of the circus acts.

Jay's father, William, became the owner of the family jewelry store in Glencoe and was the one who kept the official time for the railroad. In those days, pocket watches used by railroad men had to be checked once a week for accuracy, which was done usually on Friday. Once checked, the railroad worker would sign a form, which verified that their watch had been checked for accuracy. William would then send the form to the railroad office at the end of each week. William was an entrepreneur and became involved in other ventures in and around the Glencoe area. He supplemented his successful watch and jewelry business with selling Schubert Pianos, Home Sewing Machines, and bicycles.

One venture that he formed was a company that built roads and ditches. Being a progressive person, William purchased the first automobile in McLeod County, a 1902 Rambler with a single cylinder, chain drive, carbide lights, and no windshield that sold for $800. Ironically, a petition was filed to keep his automobile off the roads, as it frightened the horses. To promote automobiles and better roads, he sold Maxwell cars and Pope Hartford Motorcycles, using a portion of his harness shop to repair tires and vehicles.

## John E. ("Jay") Gould

William Gould's eldest son, Jay Gould, showed early signs of entrepreneurship and entertainment. This combination was a success to happen. One time as a child, Jay wanted a violin, which his father had for sale in the store. His father would only let him have the violin if he could learn to play "Pop Goes the Weasel." Displaying his showmanship at this early age, Jay wasted no time planning a program with his new violin in the bicycle shed behind the family jewelry store.

When Jay was a child, traveling vaudeville shows played at the City Hall. William Gould would bring his family to these performances.

When in high school, Jay organized an orchestra, which played at school functions and at the local church. By 1903, Jay was working in his father's jewelry store. In 1907 Jay formed the Apollo Orchestra, which performed for dances and community events. He continued to play his violin at school, church, and local events.

Jay convinced his father that the core family business, the jewelry store, should have an updated look by remodeling. Upon completion, in March 1908, Jay promoted a free concert to celebrate the event. He played the latest phonograph records. Jay promised that this would be a continuing monthly event, with the latest records and a concert to which everyone was invited.

# The Million Dollar Circus

**OUR CIRCUS MOTTO**
If we can stop one heart from breaking
We shall not live in vain.
If we can ease one life the aching,
Or cool one pain,
Or help one fainting robin
 Unto his nest again,
We shall not live in vain.

Jay E. Gould

**"BRINGING A FINE CLEAN CIRCUS TO YOUR CITY"**

The idea of the Jay Gould Circus began in Jay's theatre in Glencoe, when he put his nine children on stage to sing and dance. By 1921, all nine children were performing in vaudeville shows at churches, schools, and theatres. This developed into a road show, which led to a circus business. By the late 1920's, Jay began touring with his children during the summer as an outdoor circus.

He called it "Jay Gould's Million Dollar Circus" because he said his children were worth a million dollars to him. Jay eventually hired rides and concessions to travel with him, and it grew quickly from there. Later, Jay even put on a show that went from Thanksgiving to Christmas, performing about 26 days during this time, every day except Sunday. His circus continued until his death in 1967.

The circus was open; there were no tickets to buy for entrance. There was no "big top" to be erected at each location; rather a large central ring was setup in front of the stage for performances. Two hundred folding chairs surrounded this ring. A blue fence was erected behind the chairs. Anyone could see the circus free if they wished to stand, but for those who wished to sit, chairs were available for 25 cents each.

It was advertised as a free circus because the community, Chamber of Commerce, Rotary, Kiwanis, or other organization of each town would pay for sponsoring the circus in their area. The circus was quite an event for a community and the sponsors would benefit from the promotion. Many times the circus would coordinate the town's events with theirs. It was not unusual for the Chamber of Commerce to elect their town King and Queen using the circus' stage as a backdrop. Always planning ahead, Jay would spend the winter months marketing and setting up for the next season.

Example of a typical promotion for the Jay Gould Circus featuring Albert Nelson, this one from Burlington, Iowa:

"EX-RIPLEY STAR HERE WITH CIRCUS - Albert Nelson, one-man band who was once featured by the late Robert L. 'Believe It Or Not' Ripley, will be one of the attractions at the Jay Gould free circus, being brought to Burlington this week by the Lions Club.

The circus will have shows Thursday evening and Friday and Saturday afternoon and evening, and a downtown parade starting at 1 p.m. Friday."

A typical Gould circus would first open with Patsy Gould, who came on stage to sing "The

Star Spangled Banner," with Gloria Stibal (Jay's grand-daughter) accompanying on the calliope. Then Gary Albrecht would come out riding a white pony around the center of the ring carrying an American flag. He would then sit on his horse holding the flag until Patsy finished singing. Before Mr. Gould opened the circus he always said a prayer. The performances then began. There were high wire and trapeze acts, juggling, trained dogs and pony acts, clowns, and a midway of rides, sideshows and concessions.

Jim and Jessie Arbaugh had a flying act with four trapeze performers. Luther Dennis and his wife would perform on the trapeze over the circus, dangling from a hot air balloon.

Through Jay's natural showmanship, the circus could boast crowd-pleasing attractions. For many seasons, Jay exhibited the mummified body of John Wilkes Booth, who assassinated President Abraham Lincoln. This was one of his leading attractions for many seasons. As a child, the author remembers seeing this body at the circus.

Animals were also an integral part of the circus. Everyone liked the animal performances. One time while visiting the Gould Circus in Detroit Lakes, Minnesota, the author's father, Ray, recalled an incident with the elephant and pony that did a trick together. On this occasion, the pony was sick. The elephant would not perform without the pony. When Ray tried to pet the pony the elephant would push him away, protecting the pony. They were truly circus partners.

It is interesting to note that Jay Gould gave Lawrence Welk, nationally famous with his Lawrence Welk Show on television during the 1950's and 1960's, his start in show business. Mr. Welk did stage performances in 1923 at Jay Gould's theatre in Montevideo. The last engagement of the Jay Gould Million Dollar Circus was a setup in Elbow Lake, Minnesota, September 16th and 17th, 1967. This was Jay Gould's 60th year in show business, but he was in the Glencoe hospital. On September 23, 1967, only one week after his last show, Jay Gould died.

In that era people would dress up to see the circus. About the mid-1950's circuses begin feeling the effects of television and culture change. Leo Albrecht feels that it will never be the same as it was. First, people do not want to put the time and effort into the circus acts, and considerations of liability and vehicle insurance, workers compensation, licensure, and general liability are paramount conditions that would not allow this type of circus entertainment to return.

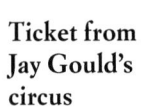

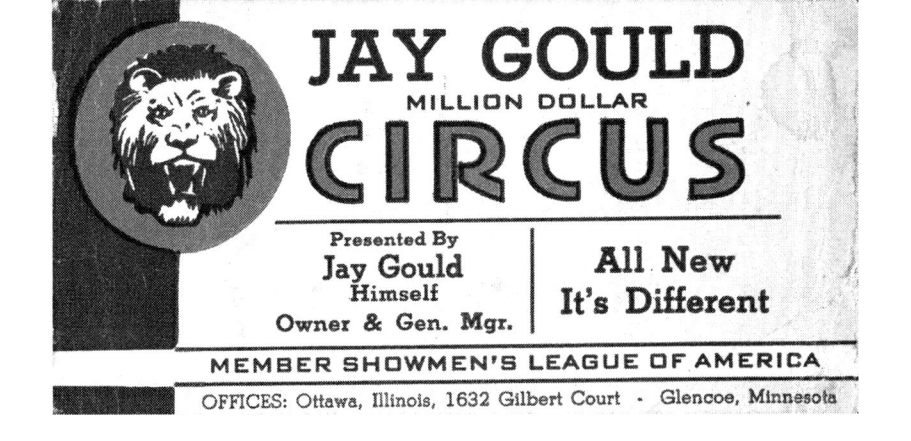

**Ticket from Jay Gould's circus**

Jay Gould
Circus stage

View of
Nelsonian
sideshow from
Ferris wheel,
St. Cloud,
Minnesota

Jay Gould's Million Dollar Circus flyer

# JAY GOULD'S MILLION DOLLAR CIRCUS
## PROUDLY PRESENTS

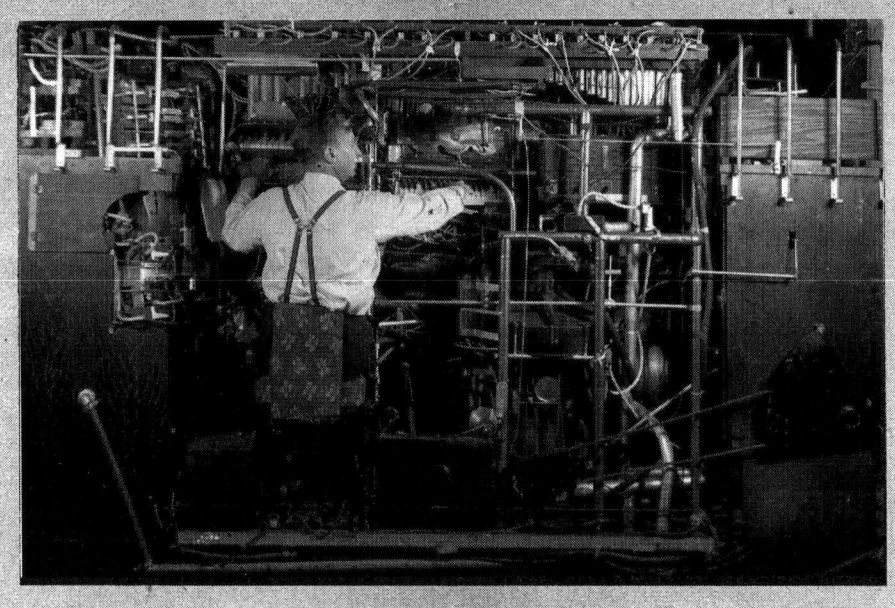

### *Mighty Nelsonian*
#### 32-Piece "One Man Band"

Albert Nelson is one man who personally conducts a 32-piece band with never a thought or worry as to musician trouble, for Mr. Nelson not only leads his large orchestra, but he also plays every one of the thirty-two instruments himself—simultaneously, if the need be.

The creation of this colossal, but compact ensemble was originally brought about by the vagaries of one musician in a string quartet that Mr. Nelson was conducting thirty years ago. After several missed rehearsals and performances on the part of the delinquent player, Albert Nelson in desperation determined to master the wayward one's instrument and substitute for him when necessary. With native musical genius, he soon set himself to the task of learning to play various other instruments in an orchestra, until he had twelve to his credit. Then the idea occurred to him: "Why not construct an entire orchestra so that one man might play it at once?"

With it in mind, he set to work at his home at Buffalo, Minnesota, and throwing his inventive genius as well as his musical ability into the project, turned out his first creation — an instrument that could play both the cello and violin simultaneously.

From then on, each succeeding year found new instruments and new combinations added to the original group, until thirty-two pieces could all be controlled and played from one position by the operator. To his finished masterpiece he gave the name "The Nelsonian."

Included in this one-man band one will find such instruments as an organ, two pianos, a marimba, several accordians, a slide trombone, a violin, a violoncello, a bass viol, snare drums and traps, guitars, a mandolin, a trumpet, tom-toms, a banjo, a ukulele and a bass drum. More than 5,000 feet of rubber tubing connects the keys of one instrument in serial to the corresponding keys of the next one.

Many of the connections, brackets and integral mechanisms of the instrument's control are made up of Ford parts. Bushings, heater and radiator hose, choke rods, speedometer cables and various brackets from Ford dealers' stock have found their way into his unusual creation.

So uniquely outstanding did Robert Ripley find "The Nelsonian," that he featured it at A Century of Progress in Chicago in his "Believe It Or Not Odditorium."

Playing "The Nelsonian" is a feat in itself. Taking his position in the operator's seat, by weird contortions, Mr. Nelson manipulates the various controls with his lips, feet, knees, fingers, arms and elbows.

Line to buy tickets to see the Nelsonian, Benson, Minnesota

Nelsonian setup

85

Truck loaded for travel, the ticket booth folded for ease of transportation

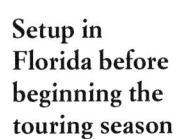

Setup in Florida before beginning the touring season

Albert being comical

Tickets to see
the Nelsonian

87

# Jay Gould's Circus Follies of 1936

**SHOT FROM THE CLOUDS!**

## SUCCESSES
### INSTANTANEOUS, MARVELOUS, UNEQUALED!
#### Prof. D. L. Dennis

**SHOT FROM THE CLOUDS**

When the monster new ballon is inflated and in readiness for its skyward flight, a large cannon is then attached, into which is placed at the proper moment, the aeronaut and his parachute. The signal is given, then up, up into the very clouds rushes the monster air ship, bearing its human freight. Then follows a sight of thrilling peril. When the balloon has attained full height the cannon is discharged, firing into empty space the aeronaut and the parachute to which he clings and descends, with terrific velocity, but absolute safety to terra firma.

GLENCOE, MINNESOTA    April-6/36

Dear Albert & Mrs: Your letter received and will say that I am surely pleased that your folks will go along and try this proposition out. I will promise that if you are not satisfied that you can leave , but I will also promise you that we will help you in every way, on setting up and tearing down, and will make every effort to set you on a lot on Main Stree where ever possible so as to get away from the pavement setting. I have ordered the mats for newspaper work and Elmer has written up a nice story about you, for newspaper work.,

Albert I realize that this is all new for you, but I am telling you this that after you have played with us one season that you will never care if you NEVER PLAY A FAIR AGAIN this is 1000 times better than fairs —more money and not the work people really spend, because its —put on the streets and there is no gate charge and they have money to spend. I am ceratinly tickled and PROUD TO HAVE You with me.

**FULL COMPANY OF 125 PEOPLE**

Revue for night show — Flying Performers — Trained Animal Acts — Clowns — Acrobats — Dance Band Balloon Ascension — 4 Laurants (Greek and Roman statues) — Circus Band — Midway (no graft, gambling or immoral shows — Marvelous Sound Bus with Perfect Sound. — Everything in keeping with the Gould Family name. — Heaven's Lofty Dome is our Circus Tent!

*Letter from Jay Gould inviting Albert to join his circus 1936*

## Touring with the Jay Gould Circus

In April 1936, Albert received a personal letter from Jay Gould inviting him to join his circus. Albert began touring with the Gould Circus that summer. For over the next two decades, Albert toured with Jay Gould. Periodically, Jay would introduce Albert and talk to the audience about Albert's One-Man-Band instrument.

The Gould Circus traveled the Midwest in vehicles painted all white. Albert had to paint his truck box, containing the Nelsonian, the same white when he joined the Gould Circus. Jay insisted that all traveling vehicles in the circus be painted with "Ducco De-Lux White." It was not long before the Nelsonian associated with the Jay Gould Circus was appearing in newspapers throughout the Midwest.

Some weeks the Jay Gould circus would perform in two to three different towns, spending two to four days in each. The circus covered Minnesota, Iowa, North and South Dakota, Missouri, Illinois, Wisconsin, and occasionally towns in Nebraska and Indiana. Summer touring started around Memorial Day and continued until about mid-September.

As written by Maynard Howe:

"The contrivance was mounted on a truck, which served as a stage at one end of the tent, which was set up over and around it. The walls on the sides and back of the truck, which protected the instruments from the weather when moving it from place to place, were removable, and when taken down exposed to the spectators three sides of the Nelsonian. Inside the tent there were no seats. A person buying a ticket at the entrance could remain as long as they desired and could walk around and watch the working of the many intricate parts from as many viewpoints as they might choose. With the audience permitted to roam at will, to move around his instrument while he was playing allowed them autonomy, and amusement in being able to watch the operator and the many moving parts create music."

Bud Conrad would sit and talk with Albert for hours. He first saw Albert play his instrument in 1933 at the Chicago World's Fair when he was only 10 years old. Bud's mother ran the snow cone concession, and Bud and his father together operated the "Airplane Bumper Game." The game was designed so that a plane fell on a nail to determine the prize associated with that nail.

To give Albert a break Bud would bring snow cones to him during his performances. Albert never cared what flavor they were; he just enjoyed the opportunity to wet his lips. Many times after Albert had played a while, Bud would ask if Albert wanted him to do a narration to the audience about the Nelsonian, and therefore give Albert a short rest. Sometimes Albert would play a few more songs, other times he would welcome the break. During the winter, Bud and his parents would visit Albert and Ida at their home in Tampa, Florida.

Albert was not always with Jay Gould. He traveled on his own with his one-man-band before he joined the Jay Gould Circus. For a short time during the summer of 1953 and several years later, Albert traveled with the Tatham Brothers Shows out of Ruskin, Florida, but always returned to Jay Gould. Albert never performed in Florida.

It was hard work being on the road over a third of the year, with setups lasting anywhere from one day to almost a week. At each stop the tent had to be setup around the truck carrying the Nelsonian. Weather was always a consideration. In the ledger records that Albert carried while on the road he would list the date, town, proceeds, what percentage was due Mr. Gould, his costs, meals and any comments for later review. There are notes stating that it was too hot or bad weather caused him not to play. Another entry mentions that his tent was destroyed in a storm. These were constant concerns and considerations while on the road.

The tent and all its related equipment had to be unpacked and set up around the truck, which with the *Nelsonian* became the centerpiece. The process had to be reversed when their stay was over. The poles, ticket booth and the picket fence, used to guide persons to the ticket booth, had to be folded and lashed to the truck. The whole process was repeated at the next setup.

After so many seasons, Albert reduced the size of his tent because of the labor involved in its setup at each engagement. His tent required two inside poles. On one post he attached a camera, which he activated during his performance to capture the expression of his audiences.

Tatham Flyer

**TATHAM BROS SHOWS**

**NELSON'S ONE MAN BAND**

Featured By

Robert Ripley At Chicago World Fair

**He Plays 32 Instruments**

6,000 ft. Rubber Tubing   50,000 Parts

**8th Wonder of the World**

**Thornton Enterprise** (c.1940's)
**Thornton Will Offer Two-Day Celebration**
**Jay Gould's Circus To Be Top Feature**

Thornton (Iowa) - Thornton is planning a two-day celebration Monday and Tuesday, with Jay Gould's circus furnishing the principal entertainment.

The program starts Monday afternoon with an hour and a half free show. At 6 p.m. there will be a softball game at the park with Thornton playing Sheffield in the junior league. At 8 p.m. there will be another hour and a half free show.

### Time for Children

The midway will open at 9 a.m. Monday. This will be children's morning with cut-rate prices for rides from 9 a.m. till one p.m.

The grand parade will take place at one p.m. Tuesday with all entries grouping at the schoolhouse at 12:30 p.m. An hour and a half free show will follow the parade.

At 6 p.m. there will be a band concert followed by an hour and a half free show.

There will be a dance at 9 p.m. with the Westerners playing old and new time music.

The midway will offer 8 rides, 8 shows and concessions for young and old.

### Circus With Clowns

The circus will include clowns, horses, ponies, elephants, monkeys and other animals.

Among the circus features will be Albert Nelson and his one-man band of 32 pieces. This includes such instruments as violin, cornet, piano, trombone, drums, bass viol, mandolin, guitar and a new Hammond electric organ valued at and insured for $100,000.

Thornton businessmen invite everyone to attend one or both days of this show.

(Reprinted courtesy of the *Thornton Enterprise*, Thornton, Iowa)

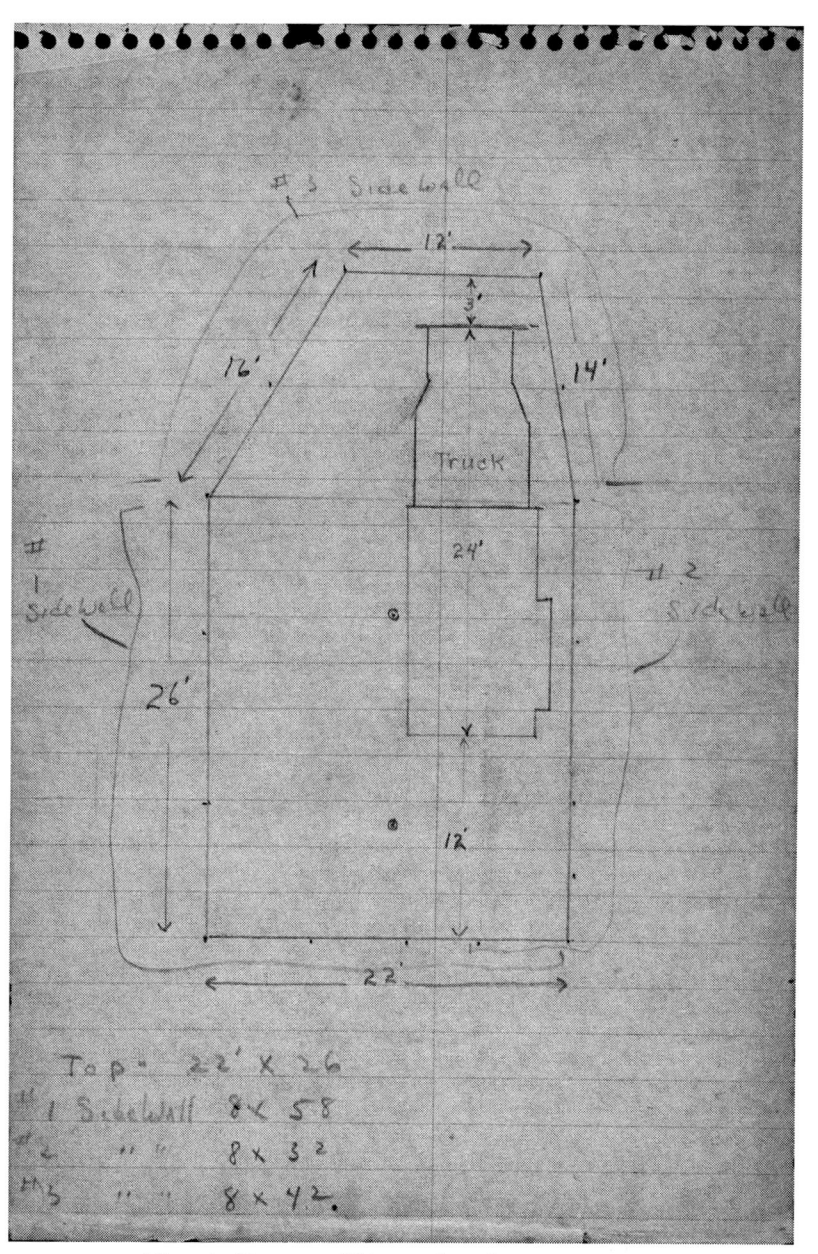

**Albert's diagram of his truck and tent setup 1950**

This page and
overleaf, top:
Albert in
operator's seat
of Nelsonian
performing c.1958

Left and next page, top: Pictures of audiences from remotely controlled camera mounted on a tent pole, Albert would activate the camera during his performances

Albert called for assistance. He had an electrical problem he could not fix and called for John Moody from Hoffman Electric in Buffalo. Albert wanted him to fly to Iowa because it would be quicker, but John refused to fly and drove instead.

| | | |
|---|---|---|
| June 25 | Eden Valley, Minnesota | "Windy & Stormy" |
| June 26 | Eden Valley, Minnesota | "Windy blew down" |
| June 27 | Eden Valley, Minnesota | "Repaired Tent" |
| July 7 | Wheaton, Minnesota | "Rain" |
| July 8 | Wheaton, Minnesota | "Stormy - rain five inches" |
| July 11 | Belgrade, Minnesota | "Rained out" |
| July 12 | Staples, Minnesota | "Too Cold & Windy" |
| August 20-22 | Knox City, Missouri | "No set up" |
| August 30-Sept. 2 | St. Petersburg, Illinois | "Cold in chest" |
| September 3-4 | Elgin, Illinois | "Cold in chest" |

Other comments listed in his travel journals:
Too hot, cold sore, sore lip, rain-too hot, no space, location poor, no lights, storm, power too low, hot weather, heat & bugs, Merry-go-round truck in front, Hammond switch troubles, cool & snow (May 30), visits of friends & relatives.

Another comment dated June 17, 1949 by Ida, "Com. Bad, Albert mad, and no setup." June 26, 1951 (Mt. Greenwood, Ill.), "Blew down - torn canvas" and June 27-28 (Kankakee, Ill.), "Tornado hit - damaged & ripped tent." When the circus set up at a drive in movie Albert would make note of that location also.

Page from Albert's travel journal dated July 25, 1951, Muscatine, Iowa

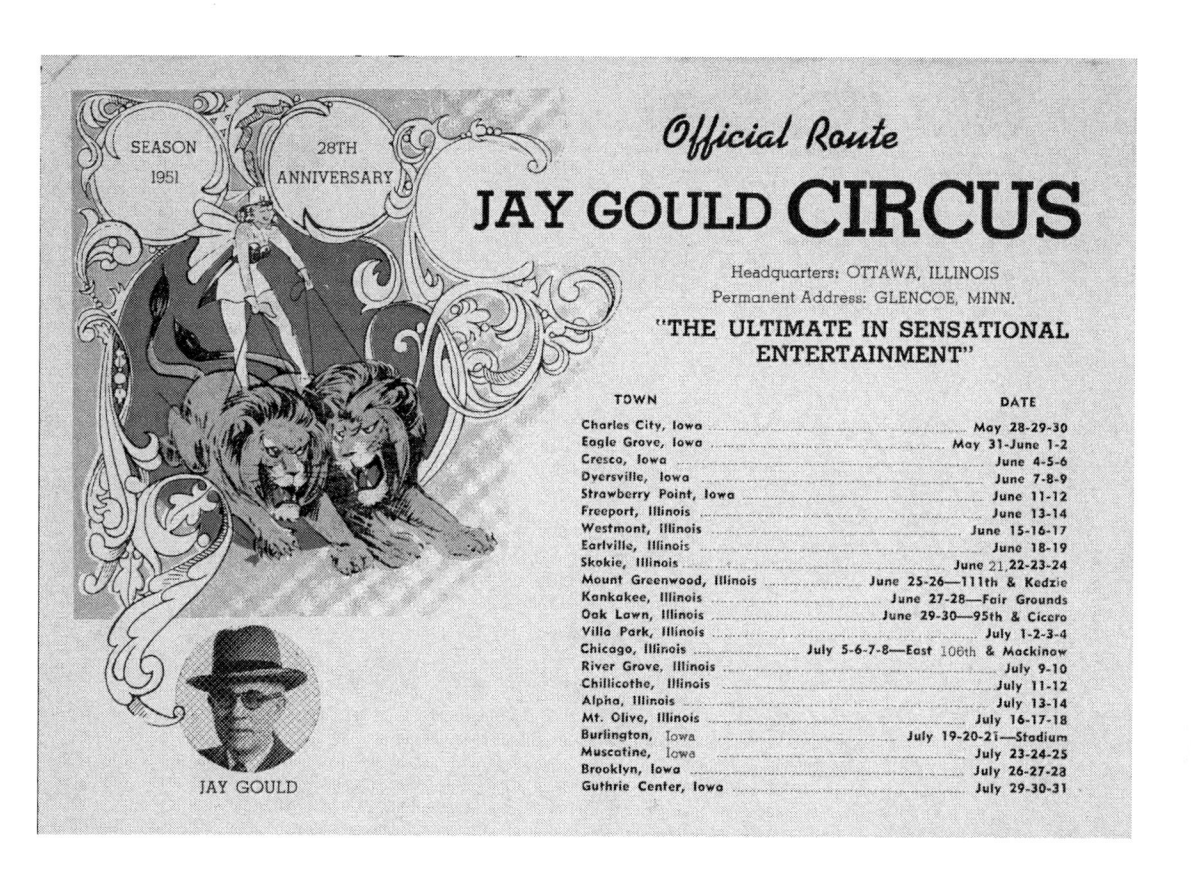

## Official Route — JAY GOULD CIRCUS

SEASON 1951 — 28TH ANNIVERSARY

Headquarters: OTTAWA, ILLINOIS
Permanent Address: GLENCOE, MINN.

"THE ULTIMATE IN SENSATIONAL ENTERTAINMENT"

| TOWN | DATE |
| --- | --- |
| Charles City, Iowa | May 28-29-30 |
| Eagle Grove, Iowa | May 31-June 1-2 |
| Cresco, Iowa | June 4-5-6 |
| Dyersville, Iowa | June 7-8-9 |
| Strawberry Point, Iowa | June 11-12 |
| Freeport, Illinois | June 13-14 |
| Westmont, Illinois | June 15-16-17 |
| Earlville, Illinois | June 18-19 |
| Skokie, Illinois | June 21,22-23-24 |
| Mount Greenwood, Illinois | June 25-26—111th & Kedzie |
| Kankakee, Illinois | June 27-28—Fair Grounds |
| Oak Lawn, Illinois | June 29-30—95th & Cicero |
| Villa Park, Illinois | July 1-2-3-4 |
| Chicago, Illinois | July 5-6-7-8—East 106th & Mackinow |
| River Grove, Illinois | July 9-10 |
| Chillicothe, Illinois | July 11-12 |
| Alpha, Illinois | July 13-14 |
| Mt. Olive, Illinois | July 16-17-18 |
| Burlington, Iowa | July 19-20-21—Stadium |
| Muscatine, Iowa | July 23-24-25 |
| Brooklyn, Iowa | July 26-27-28 |
| Guthrie Center, Iowa | July 29-30-31 |

JAY GOULD

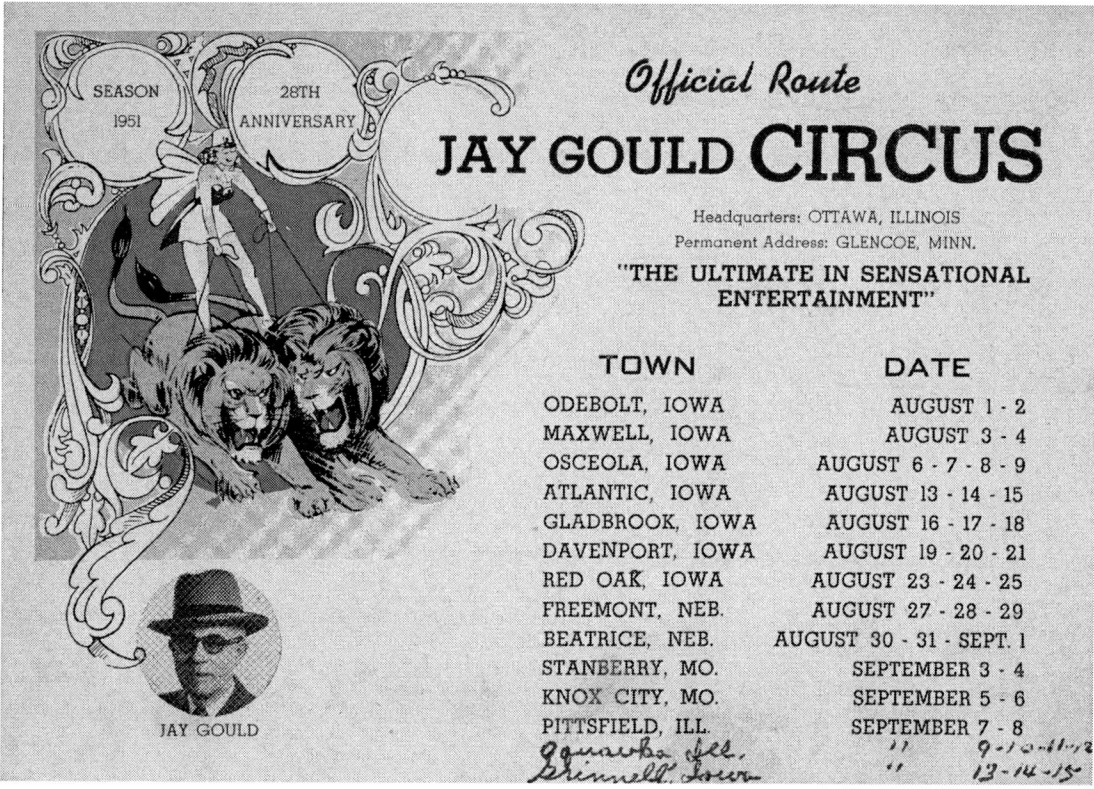

---

## Official Route — JAY GOULD CIRCUS

SEASON 1951 — 28TH ANNIVERSARY

Headquarters: OTTAWA, ILLINOIS
Permanent Address: GLENCOE, MINN.

"THE ULTIMATE IN SENSATIONAL ENTERTAINMENT"

| TOWN | DATE |
| --- | --- |
| ODEBOLT, IOWA | AUGUST 1 - 2 |
| MAXWELL, IOWA | AUGUST 3 - 4 |
| OSCEOLA, IOWA | AUGUST 6 - 7 - 8 - 9 |
| ATLANTIC, IOWA | AUGUST 13 - 14 - 15 |
| GLADBROOK, IOWA | AUGUST 16 - 17 - 18 |
| DAVENPORT, IOWA | AUGUST 19 - 20 - 21 |
| RED OAK, IOWA | AUGUST 23 - 24 - 25 |
| FREEMONT, NEB. | AUGUST 27 - 28 - 29 |
| BEATRICE, NEB. | AUGUST 30 - 31 - SEPT. 1 |
| STANBERRY, MO. | SEPTEMBER 3 - 4 |
| KNOX CITY, MO. | SEPTEMBER 5 - 6 |
| PITTSFIELD, ILL. | SEPTEMBER 7 - 8 |
| Oquawka, Ill. | " 9-10-11-12 |
| Grinnell, Iowa | " 13-14-15 |

JAY GOULD

Official Route of Jay Gould Circus 1951

Letter from Jay Gould to Albert & Ida concerning the up-coming touring season 1951

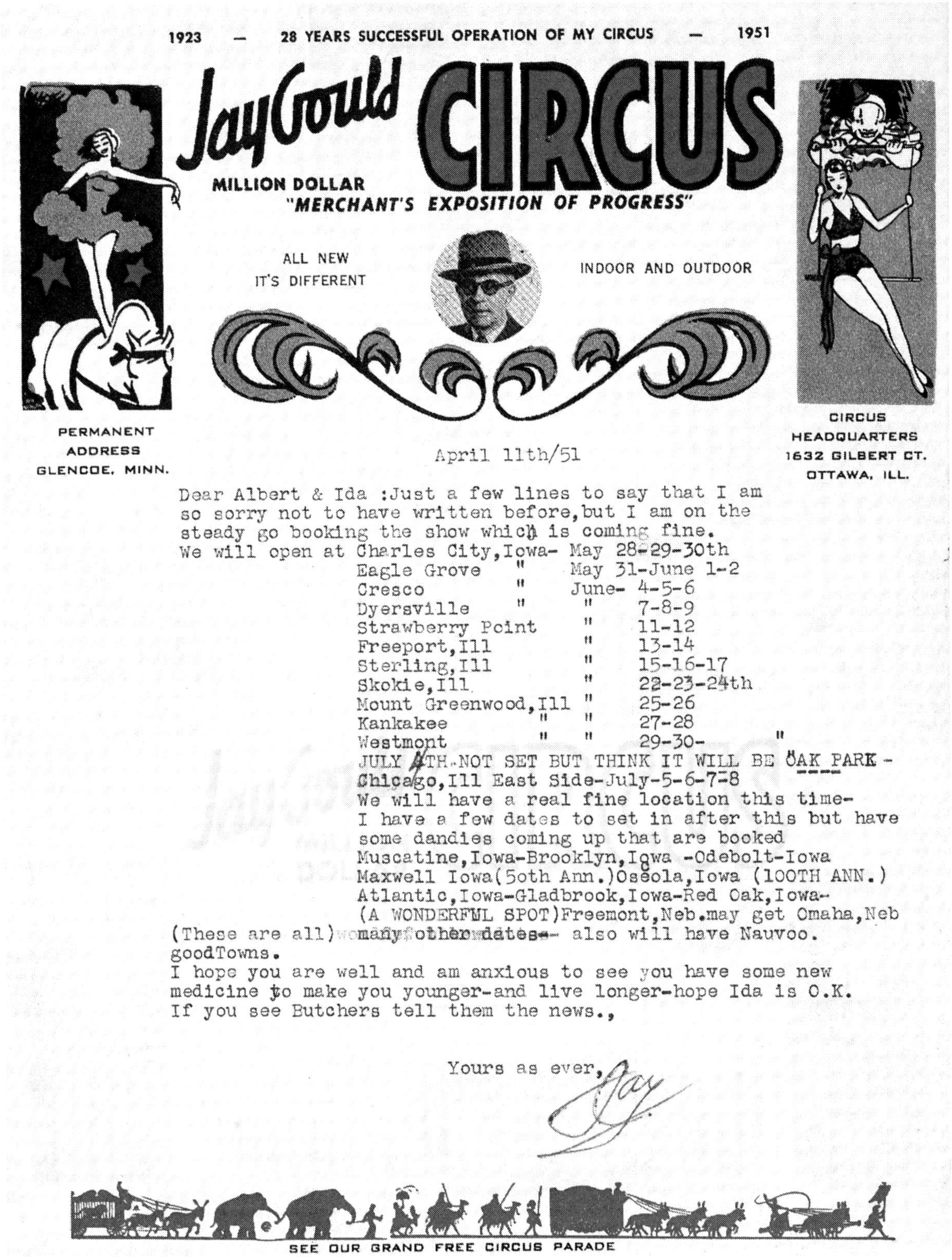

**1923 — 28 YEARS SUCCESSFUL OPERATION OF MY CIRCUS — 1951**

## Jay Gould CIRCUS
### MILLION DOLLAR "MERCHANT'S EXPOSITION OF PROGRESS"

ALL NEW
IT'S DIFFERENT

INDOOR AND OUTDOOR

PERMANENT ADDRESS
GLENCOE, MINN.

CIRCUS HEADQUARTERS
1632 GILBERT CT.
OTTAWA, ILL.

April 11th/51

Dear Albert & Ida : Just a few lines to say that I am so sorry not to have written before, but I am on the steady go booking the show which is coming fine.
We will open at Charles City, Iowa— May 28-29-30th
                Eagle Grove   "     May 31-June 1-2
                Cresco          "     June- 4-5-6
                Dyersville     "     "    7-8-9
                Strawberry Point   "   11-12
                Freeport, Ill      "   13-14
                Sterling, Ill      "   15-16-17
                Skokie, Ill        "   22-23-24th
                Mount Greenwood, Ill  "   25-26
                Kankakee         "     "   27-28
                Westmont         "     "   29-30-    "
JULY 4TH-NOT SET BUT THINK IT WILL BE OAK PARK-
Chicago, Ill East Side-July-5-6-7-8
We will have a real fine location this time-
I have a few dates to set in after this but have some dandies coming up that are booked
Muscatine, Iowa-Brooklyn, Iowa -Odebolt-Iowa
Maxwell Iowa(50th Ann.)Oseola, Iowa (100TH ANN.)
Atlantic, Iowa-Gladbrook, Iowa-Red Oak, Iowa-
(A WONDERFUL SPOT)Freemont, Neb. may get Omaha, Neb
(These are all) many other dates- also will have Nauvoo.
good Towns.
I hope you are well and am anxious to see you have some new medicine to make you younger-and live longer-hope Ida is O.K.
If you see Butchers tell them the news.,

                        Yours as ever,
                                  Jay

**SEE OUR GRAND FREE CIRCUS PARADE**

**Close up of Albert at the controls of the Nelsonian.**

# REEDLEY, CALIFORNIA

Ida Nelson, Albert's older sister, married John Larson. They moved to Reedley, California and farmed. John and Ida convinced Albert's older brother, August to move to Reedley also because there was a photographic studio for sale. August was only the third photographer in Reedley's history. Prior to his move to Reedley, August Nelson had a studio in Buffalo from 1902 to 1906. He then moved to Minneapolis and established the Arlington Studio. His wife Inga died October 4th, 1906 from heart failure. With the urgings of his sister and brother-in-law, by 1919 he had also moved to Reedley.

Albert visited his brother August and sister Ida, in Reedley, California on several occasions. On two visits, one in the winter of 1932 and again in 1934, Wesley Nelson remembers that Albert brought his *Nelsonian*. On the latter trip, Albert's brother Johnny Olson came with him. Wesley remembers also that Oscar later arrived by train. They met him at the train station. It must have been because of the limited space in Albert's vehicle that caused Oscar to come separately. He returned on the train.

On one of these trips Wesley remembers that his father Art Nelson bought a bicycle for Freddie. Albert did not want his stepson to have a bicycle. Albert was a worrier and was probably concerned for Freddie's safety.

On the first trip, Albert arrived in the fall of 1932, and left in the spring of 1933, returning again in the fall after his World's Fair experience. On both visits he brought the Nelsonian with him. As always, he was concerned for the safety of his machine. During the first visit in 1932 he stayed with August on East Street, in Reedley, they housed his instrument in a back bedroom. To make it fit, within two days they had extended the room by three feet, put down a foundation and added hinged double doors and a ramp, so it could be easily rolled into its winter lodging. Little room remained once the instrument was moved in.

As Wesley recalled:

"I remember the two visits of Albert to Reedley, on which he brought the *Nelsonian* on his truck. The first visit was when I was about five years old. The year was 1932. They wanted to put the *Nelsonian* indoors, but it was too large for the back bedroom of our home at 14th and E Street. In two days time, the entire wall of the bedroom facing the street was cut out, and 4 by 4's driven into the ground to make a foundation for the added flooring. A short roof was added and shingled, and the house was completed with the addition of clapboard siding. The house still exists, and the addition remains."

The *Nelsonian* was moved from the 1930 Ford truck and brought inside. During Albert's visit, he would sell tickets to see him perform at the house. Those coming to view the instrument would purchase tickets on the front porch, pass through the house to where Albert was playing and then go out the back door. Spectators would crowd into the bedroom to watch him play. They stood against the walls to hear the music and watch Albert manipulate the many instruments with all parts of his body. Wesley remembers the wallpaper in the converted bedroom developed a black border from being leaned against and from all the traffic that moved through to watch the *Nelsonian* be played. Later this 'extended' room became Velma's room, Wesley's sister.

Wesley remembers one time during his visit Albert took his brothers out to a local saloon

Extended bedroom of house on East Street in Reedley, California

Fresno Newspaper Ad

> **Now In Fresno... The Famous**
> **NELSONIAN**
> **ORCHESTRA**
> Operated by hands, feet, knees, elbows, chest and mouth.
>
> A 30-piece, one-man band containing 50,000 parts—from Ripley's Believe It Or Not Odditorium, Chicago World's Fair.
>
> **Concerts Beginning Today at**
> **1249 Van Ness Ave., Fresno**
> Evenings 7 to 11—Sundays 2 to 5 and 7 to 11
>
> Something entirely new and different, invented and built by Albert Nelson, who spent 23 years in perfecting it.
>
> The Nelsonian Orchestra Has NO Rolls or Records

in Reedley. August commented, "And he spent five dollars (on us)." Five dollars was a good amount in those days, it could buy many drinks. Albert's son Freddie was still in high school and attended the High School while they were in Reedley. He used to help Wesley with his homework.

Albert came again in October 1933 and stayed into 1934. While traveling through Nevada on their way to California, the truck developed a short circuit, which caused a small fire. This must have been the catalyst that caused Albert to disconnect the battery on his truck at each setup to avoid any potential harm to the *Nelsonian*.

Albert rented a storefront in Fresno and set up for performances. He had painted Nelsonian on the bricks above the awning. He was driving the 1930 Ford truck, which he replaced the next year. Wesley remembers Albert's wife Ida as being wonderful, "She was patient and kind to my sister Velma who was 11 years old, and I was 10."

Ironically, the population was slow to accept him and visit his performances because the name *Nelsonian* ended in "ian." This was an outcome from the non-acceptance of the growing Armenian population in the area since many Armenian words end in "ian."

During this visit he setup for a time in Kingsburg, California. The local newspaper reported, "The Nelsonian 30-piece orchestra, played by one man, is attracting a great deal of interest here since locating at the Joe Hamstrom repair shop, next to the theatre building, last Saturday."

Albert playing the Nelsonian in the "extended" room of the house in Reedley

Wesley and Velma Nelson in 'extended' bedroom of house in Reedley where people paid to see the Nelsonian 1933

During the 1937 visit Wesley remembers that Albert had a Brown 1937 Studebaker Dictator. The manufacturer had a problem with the generators on that model of vehicle. The generator would burn out (they did not have a voltage regulator). Albert discovered that if he kept the lights on, the generator would not burn out. These were six-volt systems at the time. During this stay they toured a National Park, Arthur Nelson took photographs and Freddie stayed home in Buffalo.

In 1940, Ida, Freddie and Ray Howe visited. Albert did not come on this trip. They came to Reedley driving a 1940 Desoto Coupe.

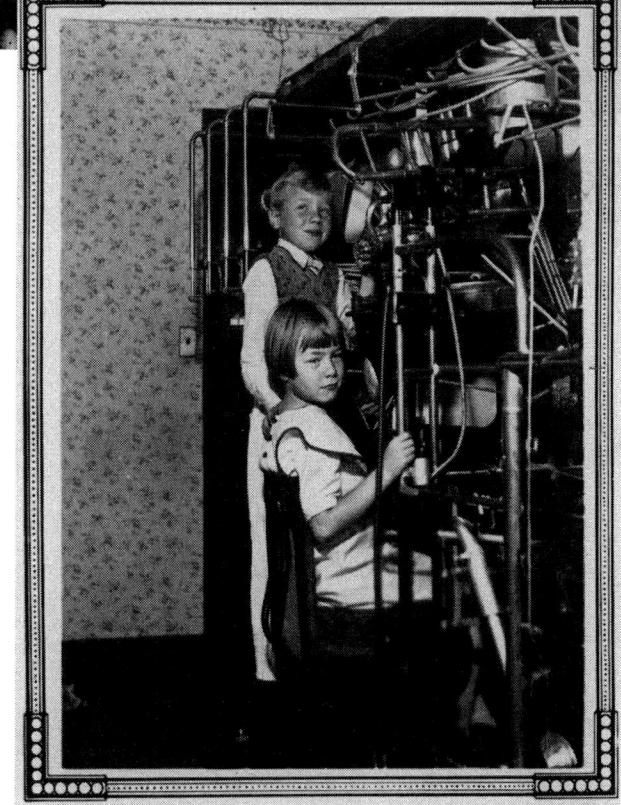

One of many stops on the way to California during the second trip with the Nelsonian 1934

Albert, Johnny and Ida at General Grant Tree in Kings Canyon National Park

The Brothers playing cards while in Reedley (L to R) Albert, Johnny, August & Oscar

# THE LATER YEARS

*My dad used to say, 'It's hell to get old.' Now that I am, I know what he meant. There are many things one wants to do, (but) it is just tough to get to doing-it. Even sending letters.*

(Written in a letter sent to the author)

**Fred Wright**

Albert continued his on-the-road seasonal life until 1958. In 1959, at the age of 75 years, he last played the *Nelsonian* in public touring for a short season predominantly in Illinois with the Tatham Brothers Circus. The *Nelsonian* was last fully cleaned and serviced by him in 1960.

One of the worst events in Albert's life was the sudden death of his wife Ida. Bud Conrad and his father were visiting Albert and Ida at their home in Tampa, Florida. After dinner, Ida said she felt tired and they all retired to bed. Because Albert and Ida's house had only two bedrooms, Albert slept in the trailer that they used when on the road. Sometime before midnight, Bud and his father were awakened by Ida's calls for help.

Rushing to her room, Bud held Ida up while his father made an emergency call on the telephone. Ida took a deep gasp and went limp in Bud's arms. He remembers, that shortly after a blowfly landed on her -- which seemed an ironic sign that she had passed away. An ambulance brought Ida to the hospital. Bud contacted Freddie but did not disturb Albert who was still asleep in his trailer. They waited until he came into the house the next morning. Bud explained to Albert that they had to call an ambulance to bring Ida to the hospital, and that he should go there right away. Albert rushed to the hospital only to find that she had died on arrival from a massive heart attack.

Albert returned home in shock. He said, "Never, never again am I going to play the band (the *Nelsonian*)", but Bud reassured him, "Oh, yes Albert, you will play it again." A little later, Bud asked Albert if he would go out and play the *Nelsonian* for him. Still in a state of shock and disbelief from Ida's passing, Albert readily agreed, "Oh, yes." Bud remembers that one of the songs he played was "Ida."

In the author's own words, "My parents would visit Olson's Point when I was growing up. I remember distinctly the last time that I saw Albert Nelson. It was at Ida's funeral in 1962 when I was only 12 years old. What I saw was not the same man who I remember visiting us in Eagle Bend. This inventor, musician, entertainer, engineer and photographer sat quietly in the family room of what was the Main Lodge at Olson's Point in its heyday, withdrawn, teary eyed, and slow to respond, but still repelled the occasional Scandinavian quips directed to him. Just days before, he had lost his wife and the desire to play the *Nelsonian*."

The author's sister related that Ida was Albert's "backbone." After her death, Albert lost interest in his machine and was reluctant to play it. Ida was always a hard worker; she helped Albert setup and teardown the tent at each engagement. Albert was always concerned about Ida. He worried about what would happen if he were gone, especially since there was 15 years difference in age between the two of them. Ida's sister-in-law Dorothy Carlson, related, "Albert died the same day as Ida. Ida got along well. She was very independent."

## 2002

Fred Wright, Albert's only child, died and wished to have a living relative be passed on the care of the *Nelsonian*.

In Fred's will he passed on the care and concern of the *Nelsonian* to the author. Although, he no longer had the legal right of ownership of the *Nelsonian*, it was his way of assuring the continued concern and care for his father's life long passion. He did this through mention in his will. He wanted to be assured that there would be another related family member who would replace him as the caretaker.

As written in his will:

". . . after my death future decisions as to the disposition of the machine (*Nelsonian*) shall be made by Gary Hukriede (address), and I transfer any interest I may have in said machine to him.

"With a heavy heart, and my promise to Fred, I put to rest the ownership of the Nelsonian by signing an affidavit to affirm rightful legal ownership of the machine called the Nelsonian One-Man-Band to the Wright County Historical Society Museum. It is housed in its rightful place, in the community from which it developed."

## 2005

Sesquicentennial of the settlement of Buffalo, Minnesota and restoration of the *Nelsonian* truck.

The author standing beside the Nelsonian in the Wright County History Museum, June 25, 2005

## Next Generations

Although the children of today are several generations removed from the era of the *Nelsonian*, they enjoy studying the intricacies of the instrument. They stand for a while tracing just one linkage to an instrument. It is also great fun for them to play "locate all the instruments" within the matrix of wires, tubes, pipes, gears, cables, etc. Active minds appear to be at work.

As one young man stated at the sesquicentennial celebration at the Wright County History Museum on June 25, 2005, as his mother called for him, "Don't bother me mom, I'm looking at the super-cool, mega instrument." Another person stated on the same day, "After seeing the *Nelsonian* as a child, this is the highlight of my whole day." Another older adult related, "As a young boy I went to one of his (Albert's) concerts with my parents, this was about 70 years ago. I was in awe about the complexity of this one-man-band and how he was able to perform all the different instruments, it is one of my childhood memories."

To another person who grew up on a farm near Little Falls, Minnesota, it was an annual event to go to the county fair, for which the children in those days waited all year. Seeing the *Nelsonian* annually marked this occasion. When the person viewed the *Nelsonian* in the museum, it brought back those nostalgic childhood memories.

Many others recalled vividly, from many years passed, watching Albert play the *Nelsonian* and hearing the music it created. They all seem to remember the energy needed and the activity of all of Albert's limbs that it involved to play the One-Man-Band.

Albert brought joy and amazement to many people. He was quoted as saying:

> "The best tonic I know for the blues is to sit and play the *Nelsonian*.
> I'd rather do this than anything. Oh gosh, I get a big kick out of playing it."

In many ways Albert was fortunate. Although he worked long and hard and experimented endlessly, he did not mind it. Through his endeavors and bearing he was able to live his dream. Few of us are as fortunate.

Albert and Ida standing by the Nelsonian tent, c. 1958

# EPILOG

"The only instrument of its kind in the world now stands still. This was the greatest of all one-man bands ever created. This Nelsonian made it possible for one person to play the music of 32 instruments.

The Nelsonian One-Man-Band is permanently housed in the Buffalo Historical Society for all to see and marvel at its creation.

Although it stands silent, it is a memorial to the great man that labored to create, by trial and error, the instruments of a full orchestra played by one individual.

I doubt that it would be possible to bring it back to what it looked like when it was at it's best, when it was almost all black with nickel trim over most parts."

Freddie Wright<br>Son of Albert Nelson

"No one will again produce harmonious music from its complicated assemblage of instruments. It is doubtful that anyone but its maker, who built and changed and rebuilt it until it virtually became part of him, could ever hope to do so."

Maynard Howe<br>Nephew of Albert Nelson

"I am glad that I had the opportunity, even at a young age to have known Albert and have the remembrance of seeing him play the Nelsonian. I am glad to be able to keep his lime light glowing."

Gary Albert Hukriede<br>Great Nephew of Albert Nelson

# APPENDICES

# Appendix A
# Family Genealogy Chart

## I. OLE and MARIT NELSON Family

**OLE NELSON**
October 25, 1833 - December 5, 1925
Born in Onneby, Sweden

**MARIT (Parsdotter) NELSON**
May 29, 1837- December 3, 1922
Born in Molnerud, Varmland, Sweden

## II. Children of OLE and MARIT NELSON Family

**Children Born in Sweden**

### 1. GERTRUDE and HALVOR OLSON
December 7, 1855 to April 1942 (86 years old)

### 2. PETE OLSON* and CHRISTINA SYLVANDER
May 7, 1858 to May 8, 1928 (70 years old)

### 3. NILS OLSON*
April 25, 1860 to 1876
(16 years old; buried in an unmarked grave near Sacred Heart, MN)

### 4. JOHN OLSON* and AUGUSTA
(John) August 2, 1862 to July 25, 1948 (85 years old)
(Augusta) May 31, 1868 to January 20, 1907 (39 years old)
John was seven years old when he immigrated to the United States with his mother. He was the owner of Olson's Point Resort in Buffalo, Minnesota.

### 5. MARIA
November 15, 1864 to October 25, 1865. Died at 11 months old.

### 6. MARIA August 16, 1866 to 1883.
At 17 years old died while the family was in Duluth, Minnesota, where Maria is buried.

sentimental significance would no longer be here became a matter of concern.

In the summer of 1973 Ray Howe approached the Wright County Commissioners with an offer to donate to the county his building, and the one and a half acres of lakeshore on Buffalo Lake at Olson's Point, providing that it would be converted into a museum for history related to Wright County. The offer was accepted with some stipulations, one being that Ray Howe, may live in the residence part of the building as his home as long as he desires to live there.

Therefore, at the time of this writing, the *Nelsonian* will have a permanent home—but no one will again produce harmonious music from its complicated assemblage of instruments. It is doubtful that anyone but its maker, who built then changed, and re-built it until it virtually became part of himself, could ever hope to do so.


EPILOGUE: These comments are mine only and may not coincide with the conclusions at which others have arrived. They are based chiefly on observations during the many trips Albert Nelson made to into Minnesota, particularly in the vicinity of Erskine. I have refrained from things of a legendary nature, confining myself to facts as I knew them, and as they appeared to me; besides, what is legendary has been well taken care of by others who were better informed in regard to such.

Maynard C. Howe, Nephew of Albert Nelson, 1974.

# Appendix C

## Newspaper Articles

Throughout his career, Albert was featured in many newspapers.

### I. World's Fair 1933

**Albert left Friday, May 19, 1933 to transport the Nelsonian to the Chicago World's Fair. The Wright County Journal-Press featured an article on Thursday, May 18th, 1933**
(Volume XLVII, Number 22, featured on page 3 and 4)

**Buffalo at World's Fair** - Buffalo will have representation at the Century of Progress Exposition at Chicago, when Albert Nelson of this city brings his marvelous *Nelsonian* musical instrument there. He will leave Friday to add his contribution to the "Believe it or Not" exhibits to be placed in display there by Cartoonist Ripley. Below is the latest picture of the newest *Nelsonian*.

**When Nelson Goes to Chicago** -- Albert Nelson, Famous Buffalo Inventor and Musician, Leaves Friday to Exhibit his Work

Among the unbelievable things that will be exhibited in the great "Believe It Or Not" show conducted by the famous cartoonist Ripley at he Century of Progress exposition in Chicago this year is the marvelous *Nelsonian* , a musical instrument that makes it possible for one man to play thirty separate and distinct musical instruments at the same time.

The story of this invention is the story of one man. He is Albert Nelson of Buffalo, Minnesota, who has invented the only instrument of its kind in all America, perhaps in all the world.

Twenty-three years ago, Mr. Nelson conducted a string quartette. One of the players often did not appear for rehearsals or performances, and so Mr. Nelson himself set out to master the instrument played by his friend. This lead from one instrument to another, until he had mastered a dozen. Then Nelson conceived the idea: why not play all instruments at one time, a full orchestra all by himself? This he set out to do, but in making such a feat possible it was necessary for him to become an inventor as well. The *Nelsonian* is not only the result of his musical ability but of his inventive genius as well.

The first *Nelsonian* had but two musical instruments, the cello and violin. One after another, new instruments were added from season to season, until now at the culmination of his great feat, there are thirty instruments in this extraordinary musical instrument that surely will take place as one of the most unusual in the whole galaxy of 'Believe It Or Nots.'

Perhaps it is one of the most complicated pieces of mechanism of the age. Set in a huge frame of nickel-plated bars and curves are the multitude of instruments, the pianos at either side, the drums, the violins, the wind instruments, and the entire host of music makers, all connected with gadgets that can be manipulated by the operator. In playing a symphonic selection, Mr. Nelson uses his lips, his feet, his knees, his fingers, arms, elbows, until one wonders whether this great artist, who turns out exceptionally fine music, is not also getting his daily physical exercise, for playing a piece on this machine is something like going through the calisthenics required in doing the 'daily dozen.'

**VI.** Pantagraph, Bloomington, Ill., Thursday, Aug. 7, 1958 (page 3)

## HE IMPROVISED
### Absenteeism in Quartet Fostered One Man Band
By Dick Streckfuss

There's a woman behind every successful man, as the women's magazines are so fond of mentioning. And by stretching the point past reason the old saw can apply to Albert Nelson, a one man band appearing at the McLean County Fair this week.

First, for the record, it should be mentioned that Mr. Nelson is a success - his act made the World's Fair, the Broadway of carnival people. If more proof is needed, he works four months or so a year and spends a quiet winter in Tampa, Fla.

**Doubles on Cello**

The woman in his life is his wife Ida, but she had no direct bearing on his career. The influential female, the one responsible for setting him on the carnival road, was the one who dated a cello player in Buffalo, Minn., back in 1904.

That female somehow kept the cello player from practice sessions with a string quartet, one member of which was Mr. Nelson.

Mr. Nelson, who at that time had a photographic studio, was no man to fly against the fatal charms of a female. As he put it, 'then I began to think, now maybe I'd better get busy and fill in on cello and still play my viola.'

The result of this thought was a double bow that enabled him to play two strings of the cello while carrying the melody with the viola.

**At Chicago Fair**

The cello-viola device led him on. 'Then I added one more and one more and one more and one more,' Mr. Nelson dais, and he could have gone on up to 32, the number of instruments that now form a weird machine with 6,000 feet of rubber hosing and more than 50,000 separate parts.

The thing grew slowly. He began playing in silent movie houses, and then in 1924 says Mr. Nelson, 'I went after it big.' That was the start of his carnival career, which has been highlighted by an appearance at the World's Fair in Chicago in 1933.

Included in the music machine are a violin, bass viol, banjo, two accordions, trombone, Hammond organ, xylophone, cello, mandola, two guitars, two trumpets, piano, orchestra bells and trap drums.

'It took me twenty years to figure the percussion system out,' he said, pointing to a maze of wires and hose and arms that looked like something out of a science fiction movie.

'I can get any rhythm I want. It would be hard for me to explain how it works; you couldn't understand it anyway.'

**Crowded Quarters**

'I can touch this here with my shoulder,' he continued, fingering a lever made of a tablespoon, 'and everything goes minor chord.'

'I have so much stuff on it, it's a job just getting squeezed into the seat to play on it.'

'But I'd rather do this than anything. Oh gosh, I get a big kick out of playing it.'

'I have to play the thing (evidently he hasn't been able to think of an accurate word for it) in house slippers because I can't handle the bass section with shoes - they're too clumsy.'

**Workout**

'There's a lot of work involved in playing it - I have to use every muscle in my body,' he said, and then, as though it had a bearing he added, 'I won't tell you how old I am because you wouldn't believe me anyway, but I'm past 60 anyway.'

'I should clean the thing, but with so many

parts it takes two good weeks. I can touch this here with my shoulder,' he continued, fingering a lever made of a tablespoon, 'and everything goes into a minor chord.'

With a housewifely groan he complained: 'My biggest enemy in the world is dust.'

'Which shows there's no escaping troubles, no matter what line of work you get into.'

(Reprinted courtesy of *Pantograph Newspaper,* Bloomington, Illinois.)


## VII. Minneapolis Star Journal -
Monday, May 20, 1946

### Fabled paperhanger Is Idle Man Beside the One-man Band

GENERALLY SPEAKING, nothing about music astonishes a musician very much. When a musician watches Albert Nelson at work, however, it's usually a mouth-ajar picture.

Nelson is owner, operator, inventor, builder, maintenance man and booker for the *Nelsonian,* the only instrument of its kind in the world. The *Nelsonian* is a one-man band. Nelson is the one man.

About this time at Buffalo, Minn., he is setting up the *Nelsonian* for this season's operations. About May 30 he starts traveling the highways, taking his one-man band - which, by the way, has 32 pieces - to fairs, carnivals and other centers of entertainment.

It is a fact that musicians have driven clear across a state just to hear him and have been mystified at the complexity of his performance. When Nelson retires, the *Nelsonian* will retire with him. It would take anyone else years to master it. It all began in 1910 when Nelson was directing a string quartet. One of the musicians proved habitually delinquent. He failed to show up for rehearsals or for dates.

Nelson decided to learn his instrument himself, and substitute when necessary. This seemed such a good idea he kept it up.

When he had learned to play 12 orchestra instruments, he thought "Why not construct an entire orchestra so one man can play the whole thing?" And that's just what he did.

At Buffalo he set about building the creation. Its first version was a machine that could play both cello and violin simultaneously.

Each year after that he added new instruments until now 32 can be played from the same position and at the same time by the operator.

The *Nelsonian* is mounted on a truck, and its instrumentation includes two trumpets, trombone, violin, cello, bass viol, two guitars, banjo, mandola, piano, four accordions, xylophone, bells, Hammond organ, trap drums and many others.

More than 6,000 feet of rubber tubing connect the operator with instruments. Many of the connections and integral mechanisms are adapted from auto parts.

To play it, Nelson sits on a stool and undergoes weird contortions with lips, shoulders, fingers, elbows, hands, chest, knees and feet. With all that equipment, he might be flying a B29. He only regrets that, with all that to do, he can't tap dance too.

(Copyright 2005 *Star Tribune.* Republished with permission of *Star Tribune,* Minneapolis-St. Paul. No further republication or redistribution is permitted without the written consent of *Star Tribune.*)

### VIII. Lake Region Press, Friday, September 18, 1981

Alexandria, Minnesota

**"The Nelsonian" one-man-band by Jon Haaven**

We're sure the name of Albert Nelson will ring a bell with some of the older residents in the Brandon area. He's the man who moved there in about 1908 and set up a photography shop. However, he is perhaps better known as a top-rate musician who appeared several times at the Douglas County Fair with his 32-piece one-man-band back in the 1930's!

Lloyd Geisness of Alexandria - the modern-day one-man band phenomenon who recently completed a 12-day engagement at the Minnesota State Fair - heard about Nelson and did some investigating. He wanted to find - among other things - the actual contraption Nelson spent five years putting together. He was successful... but a little disappointed that "The *Nelsonian*" is not on display for public inspection. (More about that, later.)

Albert Nelson was born in Buffalo, Minnesota and after living in Brandon for some seven years, moved on to Wheaton, Minnesota where he set up another photography shop. It was here that he invented "The *Nelsonian*."

He conducted a string quartet back around that time. One of his musicians regularly missed rehearsals and dates of appearances and Nelson - in desperation - finally determined to master the playing of the wayward musician's instrument so as to substitute for him when necessary. This led him to the idea of combining two instruments and this he also accomplished.

Finally - as recorded in a news article out of Hopkins, Minnesota in 1941 - the idea was born to construct an entire orchestra so that one man might play it at once. Besides inventing and building this orchestra, Nelson had to learn to play all the instruments. He played his first big creation for the first time in about 1920... seven instruments combined into one.

Each year more instruments were added until there were thirty-two pieces in all. He was eventually contacted by Robert Ripley (*Ripley's Believe It Or Not*) to appear at the Century of Progress in Chicago in 1933. The winter months were spent working on the mechanism and during the summer he and Mrs. Nelson traveled about the country exhibiting the creation... including the Douglas County Fair.

"The Mighty Nelsonian" (as it became known), was something to see and hear. Seated at the rear on a specially built seat, he manipulated the various controls, which caused the instruments to play. He used all parts of his body, lips, fingers, arms, elbows, feet and knees. Combined into one large band were an organ, a piano, a marimba, several accordions, slide trombone, a violin, a cello, a bass viol, snare drums, traps, bells, guitars, a mandolin, a trumpet, tom-toms, a banjo, a ukulele and a bass drum. More than 5,000 feet of rubber tubing connected the keys of one instrument in serial to the corresponding keys of the next one.

He did all the work himself with only his own inventive genius to guide him. No one else could play the band - no one has ever been able to figure out one-tenth of the intricate mechanisms of the controls. And as pointed out in that same 1941 article, "But after his death there is no doubt it will be placed in some historical museum where the people of future ages will still marvel at the accomplishments of one man and it will still carry the name its inventor gave it, 'The Mighty Nelsonian', as a tribute to Albert Nelson."

Well, it never quite happened that way, unfortunately. The Nelsons eventually moved to Tampa, Florida. The *"Nelsonian"* went with them. He died on Independence Day (July 4th), 1964. He was 82. A nephew in Buffalo went to Tampa and brought "The *Nelsonian*" back to Minnesota with hopes of putting it on display. Through some mix-ups in location housing the Buffalo Historical Society, Nelson's "Believe It Or Not" contraption has all but completely been forgotten.

Alexandria's Loyd Geisness found it though. On his way back from the state fair (in St. Paul, MN), he stopped over in Buffalo and discovered it tucked away in a dark corner in the Highway Department Building... covered with canvas!

It just doesn't seem right, somehow.

(Reprinted courtesy of *Lake Region Press*, Alexandria, Minnesota)

Note: Albert was born near Sacred Heart, MN and worked on his invention all his life. He died at the age of 80 years.

# Preservation and Funding of the Nelsonian

The following is a presentation for raising funds from the late 1980s (As written)

PRESENTATION FOR NELSONIAN VISITORS

(Introduce yourself and why you are here)

The video tape I am about to play is 15 minutes long. It features Albert Nelson's one man band. He called it "the Nelsonian."

There are only two known silent movies of him playing the *Nelsonian* and you will see both of them on this tape. The first film was taken by one of his nephews. The music you hear in the background is the actual music he played with the *Nelsonian*. There are also scenes of the *Nelsonian* when it was stored in the county garage.

The second silent movie was taken of "the *Nelsonian*" when Albert traveled with the Jay Gould "Million Dollar Circus." The movie is narrated by Jay Gould's granddaughter, Gloria, and her husband, Sunny Albright. At the time of this film they didn't know what had happened to the *Nelsonian* after Albert died. In the interview with them, given in August 1989, they reminisce about the *Nelsonian*.

* Turn this page over and read item about Neil Hanson.

The next part of the tape has been taken from Lorraine Ledine's tv show "The Grey Buffalo", on cable channel 8. Lorraine and Owen Moore discuss their remembrances of the *Nelsonian* and the fact that we need help in financing the restoration of the machine. For as little as a contribution of one dollar or over you can receive an artifact of the *Nelsonian*. For $10.00 or more you will receive an audio cassette of Albert actually playing the *Nelsonian* at one of his road shows. For $30.00 or over you will receive a 1/2 hour video tape of Albert Nelson playing the *Nelsonian* and interviews with Ray Howe, Vertas Kulbalski, Fred Wright (Albert's step-son) and many more. You will cherish these for many years and they make perfect gifts.

The tape ends with a plea from Jay Gould's granddaughter that we should not give up on the restoration of the *Nelsonian*."

(on back of script)

Neil Hanson is the head of the House on the Rock work shop. One of the many things they do there is to design and build orchestrations. One of the favorite orchestrations is the Blue Room, the only mechanically operated symphony of its kind in the world. Many of the orchestrations render their melodies by way of metal disc, paper rolls and metal cylinders playing everything from Tchaikovsky to ragtime. Some of the music is amplified for effect. Neil Hanson is in Buffalo to inspect the *Nelsonian* and to apply some of these techniques to make a good percentage of the instruments to move in synchronization with the actual sound of the music that Albert Nelson played. It is planned for a likeness of Albert Nelson to be seated at the controls of the *Nelsonian* if enough donations to the project are made. (end)